The awakening of movement with the ball

Editora Appris Ltda.
1st edition – Copyright© 2019 Sammir Vieira Melo
Publishing rights reserved to Editora Appris Ltda.
No part of this book can be used without compliance with the Law nº 9.610/98. Should any inaccuracies be found, they are the author's responsibility. Legal Deposit made at Fundação Biblioteca Nacional, according to laws nºs 10.994 from 14/12/2004, 12.192, from 14/01/2010.

Source cataloguing
Developed by: Josefina A. S. Guedes
Librarian CRB 9/870

M528a
2019
	Melo, Sammir Vieira
	   The awakening of movement with the ball
	Sammir Vieira Melo. - 1. ed. - Curitiba: Appris, 2019.
	   351 p. : il.; 23 cm
	
	   Includes bibliographies
	   ISBN 978-85-473-3141-2
	
	   1. Bola para exercícios. 2. Fisioterapia. 3. Yoga. I. Título. II. Série.
	
	                                                        CDD – 613.7

Book in compliance with ABNT's guidelines

Appris
editora

Editora e Livraria Appris Ltda.
Av. Manoel Ribas, 2265 – Mercês
Curitiba/PR – CEP: 80810-002
Tel. +55 (41) 3156 - 4731
www.editoraappris.com.br

Printed in Brazil

Sammir Vieira Melo

The awakening of movement with the ball

ART
Yoga, Dancing & Capoeira

FUNCTIONAL
Training

SAMIBALL®
and its ramifications

REHABILITATION
Movement therapy

Appris
editora

PUBLISHING TEAM

EDITORIAL
Augusto V. de A. Coelho
Marli Caetano
Sara C. de Andrade Coelho

EDITORIAL COMMITTEE
Andréa Barbosa Gouveia (UFPR)
Jacques de Lima Ferreira (UP)
Marilda Aparecida Behrens (PUCPR)
Ana El Achkar (UNIVERSO/RJ)
Conrado Moreira Mendes (PUC-MG)
Eliete Correia dos Santos (UEPB)
Fabiano Santos (UERJ/IESP)
Francinete Fernandes de Sousa (UEPB)
Francisco Carlos Duarte (PUCPR)
Francisco de Assis (Fiam-Faam, SP, Brasil)
Juliana Reichert Assunção Tonelli (UEL)
Maria Aparecida Barbosa (USP)
Maria Helena Zamora (PUC-Rio)
Maria Margarida de Andrade (Umack)
Roque Ismael da Costa Güllich (UFFS)
Toni Reis (UFPR)
Valdomiro de Oliveira (UFPR)
Valério Brusamolin (IFPR)

EDITORIAL ASSISTANCE
Natalia Lotz Mendes

TRANSLATION
Prof. Dr. Artur André M. Campos

PROOFREADING
Camila Moreira dos Santos

EDITORIAL PRODUCER
Bruno Ferreira Nascimento
Fernando Nishijima
Giuliano Ferraz
Jhonny Alves
Lucas Andrade
Luana Reichelt
Suzana vd Tempel

LAYOUT
Bruno Ferreira Nascimento

COVER
Canijan Oliveira

ILLUSTRATIONS
Ilustrador dos desenhos e raio-X: Sammir Vieira Melo
Fotografias da natureza: Sammir Viera Melo
Fotografias das apresentações e posturas na bola:
Ramon Ribeiro
Fotografias de apresentações: Julia Duarte (capítulo 3)
Figura: (14a) Fonte: Dharmabindu.com

COMMUNICATION
Carlos Eduardo Pereira
Débora Nazário
Karla Pipolo Olegário

BOOKSHOPS AND EVENTS
Estevão Misael

FINANCIAL MANAGEMENT
Selma Maria Fernandes do Valle

CONTRIBUTORS

Eduardo Seixas Prado,
Organizer of the book.

Physical education - UFS (2008); Master's degree in Human Molecular Science - UCB; PhD in Genetics and Biochemistry, Federal University of Uberlândia - UFU; Associate Professor in the Physical Education course of the Institute of Physical Education and Sports (Iefe) of Ufal.

Rodrigo Lacerda Alves,
Contributor to the yoga text.

Graduated in Physical Education from UFSC (Brazil) and did his postgraduate work in Activity and Health at Universidade Tiradentes – UNIT (Brazil). personal trainer and develops works in the areas of physical activities related to health and high-performance sports (triathlon). Rodrigo is a triathlete and Hatha Yoga instructor.

Rosemeire Dantas de Almeida,
Contributor to the muscles text and preface.

Physiotherapy from Universidade Tiradentes (2000) and did her postgraduate work in Postural Correction and Pain Treatment at Bahia School of Medicine (2001) in Salvador – BA. master´s degree in Physiotherapy from the University Center of Triângulo Mineiro – Uberlândia,

Brazil in 2005. PhD in Genetics and Biochemistry from the Federal University of Uberlândia (2010). Dr² Rosemeire is a Professor at the Federal University of Sergipe.

*I dedicate this work to my "Aunt Ruth" and to my family in special,
Wilson Melo, Jeane Vieira Melo and Brenno Vieira Melo and to
Gabriela Puggi and you, reader.*

ACKNOWLEDGEMENTS

Thank you God for guiding me with persistence and perseverance, never to discourage but always believe.

To my brother, Brenno Vieira Melo, and to my parents Wilson and Jeane Melo for introducing me to the Swiss ball in 2004. To my professors at the University, Rosemeire Dantas de Almeida and Professor Eduardo Seixa, for transmitting their knowledge inside and outside the classrooms in a humble way.

To Gabriela who entered in my life during the initial moments of this work, thus contributing to the fulfillment of my ideas as well as for her patience during my absences at some moments of our lives. To my friends, in special to Renan, for the initial talks about breathing. To Augustinho, for teaching me with his curiosity and learning. to the photographer Ramon Ribeiro for his great dedication to this work. To the physiotherapists Lícia Dultra for the first readings and Yuri Ramos for helping me in the beginning of the task in hand. Thank to my friends and patients from inside and outside the Avosos Institution for trusting in this work as an instrument of rehabilitation, physical activity and art.

When a human being creates a work of art, he ultimately expresses his thoughts, his feelings, his creative plan, his inspiration and entire self in a pliable material. A work of art is worth according to the qualities of the spirit expressed in itself and to the trueness in which the technique enables such expression. In creating something artistically, men resemble the Creator, and then experience infinity, perfection, and an intense movement. Three qualities are necessary for someone to become an artist. First, the person needs to have aptitude, that is, the necessary skills to master that art. Secondly, the artist must have an immense love for his or her art in order to work with effort, determination and concentration. Number three; he must have imagination and creativity to develop art through new and unknown ways.

Yesudian & Iyengar

PRESENTATION

Through my constant curiosity, I was able to live through different corporal and mental experiences with the use of the Swiss ball, which increased my attention and concentration over my body due to the high coordinating requirements to my sensori-motor apparatus, thus making me more aware of things. With this experiment of the body with the ball, I was able to feel and understand the movements, generating different levels of consciousness in the course of these experiences, reaching personal development and self-knowledge based on my sources of inspiration: yoga, dancing & capoeira.

This work is the materialization of an immense work of practical dedication and it was conceived when I was a graduate student. It came up as an attempt to better understand the body behavior on the Swiss ball through self-observation.

At first, I describe the history of the Samiball Method followed by illustrations and photographs of projects that were developed during the course of my studies and experiments. Within the history of the Samiball Method, I present a brief bibliographical review of the basic instrument - the Swiss ball, my sources of inspirations such as yoga, dancing, capoeira as well as the importance of physiotherapy. I also present the application of Samiball method in kinesiotherapy and its influence to improve performance in boardsports (surfing and kitesurfing). After that, we mention the concepts of the Samiball Method through its primary positions, basic principles, steps and ramifications. Within the Method, the author inserts a brief catalog of anatomy (drawn by himself) where biomechanics and kinesiology are brought up isolated and applied to movements with the Swiss ball and thus helping the understanding of the reader.

The book offers a range of conventional exercises (which are found on literature) and some others that are exclusive to the Samiball® method. Those exercises are based on kinesiology and biomechanics. The purpose of this diversity of movements was to demonstrate to the reader how much can we exercise in different ways using the Swiss ball. For this, the professional has to try the exercises and feel their effects, be well trained and fully aware of the transition moment because as in some sports, some specific exercises can be counter indicated and even harmful to certain people.

I hope this book serves as an instrument of studying and practicing for the different areas of body movement and adds new insights to readers, whether professionals, athletes or artists. Be it through use for rehabilitation, physical exercise, sports training, sports and art. However, let us be clear that there are movements with a high level of complexity in this book, and some of them should not be indicated for people who do not have physical or mental compatibility to perform them. However, there is a difference in this work: some movements are published for the first time and are totally inspired by yoga, capoeira, surfing and kitesurfing. These same movements are here adapted to the Swiss ball through the Samiball® Method.

Sammir Vieira Melo

2018.

FOREWORD

That's how I see him ... Sammir is a free soul.

It is a great honor to be chosen to preface this work. As a teacher, I saw and lived moments with Sammir (still a student at the time), where ideas bubbled up in his free and curious mind.

You have in your hands an excellent opportunity to grow. As knowledge brings us to extraordinary places. Now, you, reader, receive a great and honorable work that brings something innovative and of great quality. A complete literature that includes art with approaches to yoga, dancing and capoeira, and functional training with approach to surfing and kitesurfing and therapy by movement with rehabilitation.

The Swiss ball is a formidable instrument for various purposes and here we can see that it can be art, sport, movement and the cure for many pathologies. Here, you will learn how to use the ball in practice for various areas of body movement with different levels of difficulty. In this work, you will immerse yourself in an unprecedented world where the ball makes it possible to have "extraordinary flights" through movements that makes you delve into a range of exercises in several spheres of art and rehabilitation.

Here you will learn lessons that contribute to your academic, professional and personal life.

"Wisdom is the tree that gives life to those who embrace; whoever clings to it will be blessed." Proverbs 3:18

Rosemeire Dantas de Almeida

Physiotherapist - professor at the Federal University of Sergipe

TABLE OF CONTENTS

1 - THE HISTORY OF SAMIBALL - 23

    1.1 - The beginning - 24
    1.2 - The Swiss ball - 24

2 - SAMIBALL METHOD:
YOGA AS A 1.ST SOURCE OF INSPIRATION - 29

    2.1 - Yoga - 33
        Pránáyámas - 34
        Ásanas - 35
        Súrya Namaskára - 37
        Yoganidrá - 38
        Meditation - 38

3 - SAMIBALL METHOD:
DANCING AS A 2.ND SOURCE OF INSPIRATION - 41

    3.1 Dancing - 44

4 - SAMIBALL METHOD:
CAPOEIRA AS A 3.RD SOURCE OF INSPIRATION - 49

    4.1 Capoeira - 52

5 - SAMIBALL METHOD:
THE INFLUENCE OF PHYSIOTHERAPY - 55

    5.1 Kinesiology - 57
- Motion Plans - 58
- Planes and Axes - 59
- Gravity Center - 60
- Balance - 60
- Basis of support - 61

    5.2 Arthrology - 62
- Types - 64
- Spine - 68
- Movements of synovial joints - 71
- Articular analysis of the Samiball movements - 77

    5.3 Muscles - 84
- Role of muscles - 88
- Types of fibers - 91
- Nomenclature of skeletal muscles - 91
- Functional characteristics of muscles - 92

    5.4 Kinesiotherapy - 92

6 - SAMIBALL METHOD:
APPLICATION IN KINESIOTHERAPY - 95

- Published scientific articles (abstracts) - 98

7 - SAMIBALL METHOD:
THE INFLUENCE OF BOARDSPORTS - 101

8 - SAMIBALL METHOD:
CONCEPTS AND MATURATION - 107

Primary positions - 107
- 8.1 The purposes of the method - 109
- 8.2 Ramifications of the Samiball method - 109
- 8.3 Basic principles - 111
- 8.4 Stages - 111

9 - SAMIBALL METHOD: REFLECTING ON THE DISCOVERY OF THE METHOD - 117

10 - EXERCISES ON THE BALL - 121

Introduction - 121

  Seated educational exercises - 124

    Basic points - 125

    Balance exercises - 126

    Bouncer Jumper on the ball - 128

    Pelvic anteversion and retroversion - 130

    Lateral pelvic bending - 133

    Pelvic circunduction - 135

    Side shift of the glutees with trunk rotation Bodyspheres - 137

    Jumping sideways - 139

    Gluteus lateral gliding with hand on the floor - 141

    Gluteus lateral gliding with trunk rotation - 143

    Gingar with a foot posteriorization - 145

    Latero-lateral gingar - 148

    Rotacional - 151

    Balance with the ischios - 153

    Light flexion and extension of the hip with a flexed knee - 155

    Light (alternated) flexion and extension of the hip with a flexed knee - 157

    (Alternated) flexion and extension of the hip with an extended knee - 159

    Flexion and extension of the hip with an extended knee - 161

    Inferior trunk rotation with flexed knees - 163

    Inferior trunk rotation with extended knees - 165

    Feet to hand support transference - 167

    Upside down - 169

    Anterior dodge - 171

    Posterior dodge - 173

    Blessing - 175

    Hammer - 177

    Sweep - 179

    Half moon (from inside out with hand on the ball) - 181

    Half moon (from inside out with hand on the ground) - 183

    Arrow - 185

Compass - 187

Aú – Hand stop - 189

Complete hand stop - 191

Back educational exercises - 192

Stretching the abdomen - 193

Complete stretching - 195

Trunk rotational balance - 197

Rotational trunk swing with upper limbs horizontally admitted - 199

Rotational swing with trunk flexion - 201

Diagonal stretching - 203

Bridge - 205

Depression and escapular lift - 207

Balloon - 209

Chest education - 210

Basic points - 211

Supported plank - 212

Hyperextension of the upper trunk supporting the ball - 214

Plank with forearm support on the ball - 216

Superior trunk extension with hands behind the head - 218

Alternate lifting of limbs - 220

Dog looking down - 222

Alternate balance - 224

Shoulder to plank transference - 226

Trunk partial rotation - 228

Total rotation of the trunk
taking one of the upper limbs off the ground (variation) - 230

Abdominal sitting on the heels - 232

Hyperextension of lower trunk - 234

Lateral flexion - 236

Peacock - 238

Knee Education - 240

Basic points - 241

Bouncer jumper - 243

Circunduction - 245

Snail (A) slight hip extension and flexion - 247

Snail (B) with a complete hip and knee extension and flexion - 249

Scapular protraction and retraction - 251

Abdominal with forearm on the ground - 253

Plank with lower limbs movement - 255

Unipodal balance with trunk rotation - 257

Partial and complete trunk rotation - 259

Trunk rotation with lower limb abduction - 261

Êkapada Kákasána-Arabesque - 263

Trunk rotation with elbow flexion and lower limb extension - 265

Plank with trunk rotation and extended lower limbs - 267

(Rája Kakásana) shoulder flexion and extension - 269

Plank with lower trunk lateral flexion (lumbar spine) - 271

Plank with elbow flexion and extension - 273

Plank with shoulder flexion and extension - 275

(Vrishkásana) hip flexion and exyension - 277

Plank with hip raising - 279

Plank with hip raising and flexed shoulder at 180 degrees - 281

Scorpion (horizontal abduction to shoulder flexion) - 283

Development (elbow flexion and extension with a raised hip) - 285

Knee on the ball - 287

One foot stance with knee - 289

Squatting on the ball - 291

Orthostatic position on the ball - 293

Pendulum - 295

Wall Education - 297

Standing on the sole of feet - 298

Hip and knee flexion-extension - 300

Rotacional - 302

Hip and spine flexion - 304

Abdominal with spine rotation (variation) - 305

Supine on the ball and feet on the wall - 306

Supine hip and spine flexion - 308

Foot raising with hand support - 310

Upside down spider - 312

(Sarvángásana) leg raising with hip abduction - 314

Sail - 316

Board Education - 318

Hand rail stretching - 319

Layback simulation - 321

Grab rail simulation - 323
Change of directions - 325
Basic jump - 327
Basic jump with tail grab - 329
Jump with grab rail - 331
Grab rail variations - 333
Board approximation and distancing - 333
Abdominal knee flexion-extension kite/surf - 336
Side shift - 338
Hand rail air simulation - 340

11 - REFERENCES - 343

CHAPTER 1

THE HISTORY OF SAMIBALL

Samiball is characterized by a technique and body and mental expression that makes use of body exercises. This technique distinguishes itself by having a new model of Swiss ball use (base instrument) as a complementary object to the body. Despite using many existing exercises on the ball available at the literature, some of the other exercises were initially inspired and adapted from *yoga*, *capoeira* and *dancing* (the sources of inspiration for this method) and later of sports (like surfing and kitesurfing). These movements can be used for rehabilitation, prevention, training and for art as well.

The construction of this proposed method happened during my professional training in the area of Physical Therapy. Consequently, in this first chapter, I will address the construction and the evolution of the proposed method. Moreover, as they happen to be the basis of the Samiball Method, a reassessment of the basics of the Swiss ball utilization were also made as well as a review of the initial inspirational sources to the method: yoga, dancing, capoeira and their influences to physical therapy and boardsports. As you go about reading the book, you will find it useful to come back to this chapter and refresh your memory on these basics from time to time.

23

1.1. THE BEGINNING

My contact with the base instrument

Everything started in late 2004, when I was a Physical Education graduate student and received a yellow Swiss ball, size 75 cm. (Fig. 1) as a gift from my father. I inflated right away and on the first few days, I looked at it and was not interested at the ball at all. Some days went by and I finally had the first interest on it.

Fig. 001

At this time, I started having interests in academic studies, yoga practices and the frequent use of the Swiss ball, I had the curiosity of experiencing some movements on the ball. These experiments evolved to the point of becoming the base instrument for the method. To better understand the importance of the ball to the method, we present a brief review of this instrument.

1.2 THE SWISS BALL

Fig. 002

The ball started being used for therapeutic and preventive purposes in late 1950s and early 1960s when a Swiss pediatrician Elberth Köng and physiotherapist Mary Quinton used large balls for neuromuscular reeducation treatment in children through the Bobath Method. However, as for therapeutic exercises, the physiotherapist Susanne Klein-Vogelbach created the "Swiss" ball around 1963. Aquilino Cosanie, a toy manufacturer, manufactured it in Italy (MARTINS, 2007).

After completing her course at the Bobath method in Switzerland, experienced physiotherapist Joanne Posner-Mayer worked closely with specialists trained by Susanne and Maria and took her work to the USA. However, the ball that was used by North American therapists and first seen in Switzerland in the early 1960s was named "Swiss Ball" (CRAIG, 2005; MARTINS, 2007).

In the mid-1960s, the Bobath couple used it as a method of rehabilitation. After being introduced to the ball by the couple, Beate Carrière, began to use it in children to facilitate the movements between 1967 and 1984. She then used with adult patients to treat orthopedic and neurological dysfunctions with the aim of training some lost functions, balance, muscle tone and visual-spatial coordination (CARRIÈRE, 1999).

Patients with orthopedic and neurological problems had some dysfunctions such as of tonus, reduction and limitations of range of motion (CARRIÉRE,1999). These functional impairments and limitations are diagnosed and submitted to physiotherapeutic treatment in order to improve function and prevent disability. Therefore, the ball can be used as a rehabilitation and training tool.

These balls within the treatment program, providing fun for individuals of all ages, as well as improving alignment, flexibility, tone, strength, coordination, balance, and proprioceptor stimulation can be used as a therapeutic resource (AMANAJÁS, 2003).

Since the 60s, the Swiss ball has been used in sporting spheres mainly in Germany and Switzerland with the objective of developing flexibility, strength, balance and coordination. Other benefits are increased muscle activation, co-contraction, and dynamic stability (GARCIA, 2000 *apud* LOPES, 2006).

In the United States in 1980, Paul Check, a sports coach, became a pioneer in using the Swiss ball as a performance tool while working on the rehabilitation and conditioning of Chicago Bulls' elite athletes (MARTINS, 2007).

That is why the Swiss ball is used for rehabilitation, prevention and training, up to the point of becoming a tool for well-known methods, in special – Pilates.

Gyms started introducing the Swiss balls into stretching, conditioning, and strength exercises. Although a relatively new object, it has been explored in health, with new training sets, such as "functional training – T.F.".

According to Verderi (2008), the T.F. was brought to Brazil in 2002 and is characterized as a training method that integrates several physical capacities of the individual (strength, flexibility, balance, speed, resistance and coordination).

In association with the results achieved with the Swiss ball use in different areas, its several sizes and vivid colors, its soft aspect and pleasure to use and, at last, for being a new instrument in the health studies; academic literature has been one of the great vehicles to make the Swiss ball increasingly popular. This popularity thus contributing to its functional growth.

Precautions

- Insecurity: If you are not confident in doing the exercise by yourself, do not perform it or ask for help from your counselor.

- Pain and discomfort: If any exercise causes you pain or discomfort, stop or reduce the intensity immediately.

- Crianças: avoid leaving balls alone with children and avoid accidents.

- Gestantes: pask permission to a doctor before starting the exercises on the ball and be guided by a specialized professional to follow the program at all times.

- Idoso: naturally, older people have balance deficits due to aging, thus presenting more limitations, so be more careful in teaching and passing on the movements.

Ball Pressure

When the ball is well inflated, it will require greater body balance and will be easier to roll with a lower base of support (BS) as you have a smaller ball area in contact with the ground. In contrast, a not-so inflated ball will need less balance and it will be more difficulty to roll as the base of support will be bigger inasmuch as the ball contact with the ground (MARTINS, 2007).

Ball Sizes

It will depend on the type of activity, goal and kind of patient or person to use it. It is related to weight, height and the length of the individual (MARTINS, 2007).

Ideally, when you are in a sitting position on the ball, your spine should be erect and your hips and knees at a 90° angle.

There are several sizes of balls: 45 cm, 55 cm, 65 cm, 75 cm, 85 cm, 95 cm and 120 cm in diameter.

CHAPTER 2

SAMIBALL METHOD®: YOGA AS A 1.ST SOURCE OF INSPIRATION

It all started in my own room as I tried to get on my knees on the ball (Fig.3). After several attempts, I soon realized how much the balance on the ball was directly connected to breathing and the breath tied to mental balance to generate concentration on the ball. This conclusion came from body consciousness acquired through my experiences with Yoga.

Fig. 003

Fig. 004

My relationship with yoga started in Florianópolis in 2003 (Fig. 4 – Mayurasana posture). I tried it and I have been practicing it since then, I keep on the pursuit of self-knowledge while taking some courses and experiences that contributed to my discoveries.

Fig. 005

I began my studies figuring out how I could stretch a certain muscle group on the ball (Fig. 5). I had a wardrobe that, with a mirror on its door, served as a reference to see myself. From then on, I started drawing poses in a notebook to not forget them. (Fig. 6)

Fig. 007

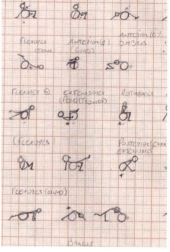
Fig. 006

On a certain day of practice, I started adapting Yoga poses (Fig. 7 Mayurasana adapted for the ball) to the ball and in each practice new ways of adapting the positions were revealed.

As I got more and more acquainted with the ball, I expanded my movements and surpassed my limits and gravity. As days went by, amidst my dedication and concentration in my studies, I began to understand there were 4 basic poses on the ball and that all other poses are derived from it. That's why I named them Primary Positions (I'll go back to those positions later). This enabled me to connect

Fig. 008

one Yoga pose (Fig. 11; Rája Kákasana adapted for the ball) to another, which made me think about the transitions.

From one moment, by connecting one primary position to another, I realized that I was doing some sort of improvisation on the ball, connecting some Yoga poses without losing contact with it, hence coming up with a new approach to stretching. (Fig. 8)

But it was during the final stage of a Yoga practice, that I had a moment of creativity and visualized a new sequence of exercises on the ball. At the meditation moment, it poped on my mind the idea of making a Sun Salutation pose on the ball (Fig. 9 and 12), with no drastic changes in the biomechanics of the poses which permitted a total new line of movements on the ball.

Fig. 009

The relationship between Yoga and Samibal method is precisely at the ability of performing some yoga poses with the Swiss ball and in total association with breathing exercises and meditation techniques (Fig.10).

Fig. 010

Fig. 011

In the Samiball method there is a salute to the sun which is performed in conjunction witc the Swiss ball (shown in fig. 9 and 12), thereby anabling a different and challenging practice in which the body tends to settle on the ball.

Fig. 012

Through the next topic, we have a review of Yoga so that the reader can understand the importance of this first source of inspiration for the method, as well as to get familiar with some Yoga terms and techniques.

2.1 YOGA

Yoga is a practice philosophy, a spiritual discipline originated in the Hindu culture and it has been around for more than five thousand years. Since the beginning, its main objective is to lead the practitioner to a state of consciousness that is beyond ordinary consciousness. In Sanskrit[1], this state is called samadhi, and it can be translated as "ecstasy." In short, the yogin (a yoga practitioner) aims at transcending his/her human condition by aspiring to a dimension that is beyond ordinary reality. This dimension has been called God, the Supreme Being, the Absolute, the Self (transcendental), the Spirit, the Unconditioned and the Eternal (FEUERSTEIN, 1998).

Yoga originated in a civilization called Indo-Saraswati, now India, and is part of the cultural universe of Hinduism as one of the paths, one of the spiritual disciplines of self-knowledge. The word yoga is etymologically derived from the verbal root "Yuj" which means "to conjugate, to join, to yoke" (FEUERSTEIN, 1998; HERMOGENES, 2001).

In this sense, yoga encompasses a broad universe of values and techniques that aim at transcending human condition, through body and mental exercises, in search of the divine essence that lives within each one of us. Recent researches have shown the effects of these techniques on practitioners' body and mental functioning and concluded that this age-old practice of self-transcendence can be used as an antidote to most diseases from modern era.

There are many styles of yoga described in the literature, but the main schools are: Karma yoga, yoga of action, that is, you must fulfill the action that fits you, therefore, action is superior to inaction

---

1 Ancestral language of Nepal and India. Although it is a dead language, Sanskrit is one of the 23 official languages of India as it demonstrates an important liturgical use in Hinduism, Buddhism and Jainism.

(FEUERSTEIN, 1998).; Bhakti Yoga, connected to a strong devotional character, the emotional power of the human being that is purified and channeled to God (FEUERSTEIN, 1998). We also have Jnana yoga, the intellectual Yoga with its liberating wisdom and Raja Yoga or Patanjali yoga that refers to the system of yoga systematized by Patanjali himself and recognized as a darshana (vision, point of view) of Hinduism.

After the aforementioned classical yoga of Patanjali, a new method came up and it was named hatha yoga, a post-classical yoga methodology with its philosophical bases in Vedanta and Tantra. Without a shadow of a doubt, it is the most known and popular method to date. It was known as "Yoga of strength", or "Yoga of the diamond body", since for hatha yogin, the importance coming from the development of body's potentials becomes essential to achieve the goal of Yoga. That is, we use the body as a starting point for investigations of subtler realities of the human being and seek self-knowledge through physical poses. We are not referring to the preservation of a beautiful, aesthetic body within the standards of beauty of current society, but rather to the construction and preservation of a strong, healthy and disease-free body, avoiding disrupting the daily sadhána (spiritual practice) which is indispensable for success in yoga practice. To achieve this, the referred method uses pránáyámas, asanas and corporal purifications aiming at the preparation for meditative practice.

PRÁNÁYÁMAS
Breathing Exercises

Pránáyáma is capturing, expanding and mastering bioenergy through breathing exercises exclusively from yoga. The word *pránáyáma* derives from two Sanskrit terms; *prána* that means bioenergy, vital force, breathing, vitality and *ayama* which means expansion.

Breathing is always associated with mental states. This can be proven by observing the breathing of a furious person in contrast with a quiet person. Probably the first one's breathing will be agitated while the second will be calmer.

Iyenga (2001) states that wise yoga masters defended the practice of pránáyámas as the very core of yoga, because they knew the connection between breathing and consciousness.

According to Eliade (2000), there is always a relationship between breathing and states of consciousness. Breathing serves as an instrument of unification of consciousness, that is, by breathing and slowing it down, one can access inaccessible mental states in wakefulness. Consequently, breathing control is an effective method for altering our emotions and seeking better states of concentration. We can achieve that through training and mastering breathing techniques, calming our minds as well as making it sharper.

ÁSANAS
Yoga Poses

According to Hindu history, the God Shiva was a dancer who improvised some instinctive body movements that were extremely sophisticated and very beautiful thanks to his virtuosity. This body language had no relationship to ballet, but it had some undeniable inspiration in dancing. It is likely that yoga poses originated from this dance.

According to the Hindu tradition, Shiva - founder of yoga, is also Nataraja, (Nata = dance; raja = king) the Lord of Dance. He initially taught his wife Parvati the poses in a number that matched all species of animals (IYENGA, 2001; 2003). Needless to say, cats are great practitioners of Asanas. (Fig. 13).

Fig. 013

According to Feuerstein (1998), *Gerandha*

Samhita states that *Shiva* taught 84.000 poses, of which 32 are considered more important for the *yogin*, whereas the Hatha yoga Pradipika describes only 16 poses. Some current yoga books describe more than 200 poses. In Brazil, we have a systematization of *asanas*, which describes 108 families with more than two thousand variations in total. According to *Patanjali*, *asanas*, are only the sitting positions in classical yoga. *Dhyanásanas* are used as a support for meditative and respiratory techniques. From the onset of *Hatha Yoga*, it also refers to the various body poses, and then designates psychophysical exercises to harmonize the vital force, balance and heal the body. All these "asanas" present precise geometric and architectural forms and that is why they become another element of fine arts (IYENGA, 2001).

Due to these characteristics mentioned above, the ásanas when perfomed in Sun Salutation become the most visible part of the technique, yoga generally calls attention of the lay public that associates it with acrobatic gymnastics from the East. This leads to a reductionist and erroneous understanding of yoga by most people who see it as just another way of exercising the body; a method of physical conditioning with a bit of contortion. One must remember that performing difficult poses or being gifted with great flexibility does not mean spiritual evolution. The most important is the mental attitude that is cultivated while staying in each pose.

> The mastery of the asanas and pranayamas helps the practitioner to release the mind from the body which automatically leads to concentration and meditation (IYENGA, 2001, p.23).

SÚRYA NAMASKÁRA
Sun Salutation

Sun Salutation (Fig.14) is a series composed of a group of asanas in sequence and that is used by man to revere the sun-God. There are different ways to perform this salutation and they vary according to different yoga lines.

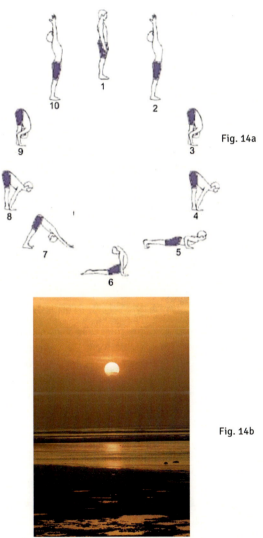

Fig. 14a

Fig. 14b

YOGANIDRÁ,
The relaxing from yoga

Yoga nidra means yoga sleep and it is a conscious relaxation technique developed by Swami Satyananda Sarawasti. It provides a deep physical, mental and emotional relaxation and aims to take practitioners to a state of consciousness that is between deep sleep and wakefulness. According to Le Page (2007), it is a state on the threshold between sleep and meditation and permits the contact between subconscious and unconscious to occur spontaneously, making the yogin more receptive to mentalization and releasing all his/her creative potential.

For the practice of yoga nidra one must be in shavásana, posture of a corpse, in which the body remains lying supine. The sankalpa, or inner resolution, is another element present in yoga nidra. It is a short sentence and full of meaning that must be repeated mentally for some transformation on the practitioner. This technique proves to be an effective tool for the self-transformation of a yogin as well as a way of accessing deeper sectors of consciousness in order to prepare the mind for the practice of meditation.

Today relaxation is a widely used technique in hatha yoga classes as it meets the needs of modern men who are fatigued and stressed by the rat race seeking for alternatives to relieve the stresses. Filho (2005, p. 179) lists some benefits of relaxation practice:

> [...] it provides a fast and complete recovery of fatigue of any kind, it cures physiological disorders produced by excessive work and tension as well as it harmonizes mental processes by reducing the feverish activity of vrittis (mental waves); clearing the barriers of a tensional nature.

MEDITATION

Meditation is undoubtedly the most important and oldest technique of yoga because it is the most concrete way to access deeper sectors of consciousness and reach samadhi. There is much controversy regarding the concept of meditation. According to Kupfer (2001, p. 82) "to meditate is to stop the flow of thoughts in a contemplation of some given object until it consciousness saturates with it. By stopping the turbulence of vrittis,(waves of thoughts in mind matter) buddhi, intuition manifests itself". For Patanjali, "…the unidirectionality (ekatanata) of ideas (present in consciousness) in relation to the object of concentration is meditation (dhyana)" (FEUERSTEIN, 1998, p.286). These concepts differ greatly from the meaning that the word meditation has gained in the Portuguese language. According to Rocha (1996, p. 400) meditating is: "Think carefully. Reflect. Consider carefully. To ponder." One may realize that meditation gained the meaning of thinking, reflecting, that is, increasing the activity of the mind, which seems contrary to the true sense that meditation has in the spiritual disciplines that originated it.

There are several techniques that aim to lead the practitioner to experience meditative states such as: concentration on an object, a visual image, a mantra, some body part, etc. However, what is in common is the reduction of the flow of thoughts through the increasing concentration on the object contemplated.

> Through deep meditation, the knower, the knowledge and the known becomes one. The seer, the vision, and what is seen have no existence apart from one another. It is like a great musician becoming one with his instrument and the music that comes out of it. So, the yogi is in his own nature and understands his identity (Atman) as being part of the Supreme Soul within himself. (IYENGAR, 2003, p 20).

Nowadays, meditation is not only used by the spiritual disciplines of India; Buddhism, Taoism, Cabbalism and Christian traditions among others also make use of it for meditation techniques.

Suggested Readings:

A Árvore do yoga, Iyengar, B.K.S. Ed. Globo, 2001.

A Luz do yoga, Iyengar, B.K.S. Ed. Globo, 2003.

Yoga prático, Kupfer, P Ed. Dharma, 2001.

CHAPTER 3

SAMIBALL METHOD®: DANCING AS A 2.ND SOURCE OF INSPIRATION

Almost at the end of 2006, I met Gabriela (Fig.15). She was taking ballet, modern and contemporary dance classes for more than nine years. We soon started to live and experience everything that I had experienced alone. I started to explain a few moves for her and from these meetings, in early 2007, I was introduced to other dancers and a choreographer.

Fig. 015

The World Dance Day was approaching, April 29, 2007, and the Tobias Barreto Theater in conjunction with the State Secretary for Culture organized some performances. Then it came an invitation to perform at the Show (Fig.16, 17, 20), including a choreography on the ball. During this period, all dancers took stretching classes, contact improvisation, contemporary dance and some instructions from my experiment (Yoga applications on the Swiss ball) during some months as a preparation for the presentation itself. After this, I realized that my experiment was indeed a kind of dance that fit the contemporary type and we could confirm that through photographs and videos. From there, we built other choreographies and in May of the same year, I received an invitation to perform at some Universities.

Some months later, during the Northeastern Meeting of Physiotherapy (Eneefisio) Students in July, I received another invitation to perform again at the opening (Fig. 18). As it was a meeting of physiotherapy students, I held a workshop entitled Samiball. Years later in 2009, I was invited with two dancers on World Dance Day (April 29) to other presentations also held by the State Secretary for Culture (Fig. 21). At the end of the same year, some university students in Sergipe invited me for more presentations (Fig. 19).

It was from these presentations that I came to the conclusion that the relationship of dancing with my experience, lies in the dancer's ability to draw up and perform free movements using the Swiss ball as a complementary part of the body. This

Fig. 016

Fig. 017

Fig. 018

Fig. 019

Fig. 020

Fig. 021

could be characterized by a contact improvisation of the body on the ball, using music and it also could be considered as contemporary dance, marked by free movements and no rules and bringing spontaneity.

Therefore, the ball is an element of a circular shape that allows movements in the four planes in a plastic, continuous and harmonious way. There is no break in the movements or loss of contact from the body with the ball in an abrupt form. The result, therefore, is a contact improvisation (body / ball), where the dancer performs a range of movements in several planes and axes.

The following theme reports a brief review of dancing so the reader can understand how dancing was part of the method and served for the development of it and becoming the second source of inspiration.

3.1 DANCING

Dancing has always been present in the oldest social organizations, either to celebrate the forces of nature or changes of the seasons. It is as old as human beings are and can be understood as a copy or an interpretation of essential movements and rhythms to the human being. For anthropologists and archaeologists, primitive men danced as a way of demonstrating physical exuberance or as a simple attempt to transmit some information, being used later as a form of ritual. Through their repetitive and rhythmic gestures, men used dance to warm their bodies before hunting and combat (CAMINADA, 1999; PORTINARI, 1989).

It is widely known that dancing came up from the need to express an emotion, a particular fullness of being, an instinctive exuberance, a mysterious appeal that reaches even the animal world, however, men were the only ones to elevate it to an *Art* category as a result of their conscience. Gradually, dancing started to submit itself to disciplinary rules, establishing a concern with an aesthetic coordination of movements, natural and instinctive to the body until then (CAMINADA, 1999).

Dancing is understood as an expression through body movements that transcends the power of the word or mimicry (GAURAUDY, 1980 *apud* RANGEl, 2002).

Dancing produces a visual and/or kinesthetic discharge of energy in time and space that is generated by muscular responses to stimuli. Their structures and styles can be analyzed through time, rhythm, dynamics and use of the body (NEVES, 1987 *apud* RANGEL, 2002). One cannot perform dancing without six basic elements: time, space, sound, movement, form and energy. The reason for this is when a movement is performed within a certain space, whether limited or not, presenting either a round or rectilinear shape, rhythm or energy it takes place in a period of time independent of our will (RANGEL, 2002; BARRETO, 2004).

As it was mentioned above, rhythm is an essential element in dance and it permits men to express themselves making use of all parts of the body and placing them in the service of the compass, so that, the intoxicating character of dance is emphasized to reinforce the rhythm (CAMINADA, 1999).

According to its movements, Dancing classifies them as harmonious and disharmonious to the body. The harmonious ones display dancing types considered open or of expansion; closed or exclusionary; seating type; spinning and twisting. The goal is to overcome the body's natural limitations by trying to break the bonds of gravity with upward and forward movements generated through pleasure and ecstasy stimuli. Disharmonious movements to the body may be convulsionary pure, attenuated, malaial or morbid ones (CAMINADA, 1999).

As for types, dances can be imitated, abstract and with or without images. Concerning the styles of dance we can highlight some as classical, neoclassical, free, modern, contemporary, improvised-contact, etc. (CAMINADA, 1999; RANGEL, 2002).

Fig. 022

Classical dance originated in the 17th century, and sought to demonstrate a beautiful posture, lightness and technical rigor when performing its movements, demanding from dances movement domains not so familiar to most human beings. Neoclassical dance came up in the late nineteenth century

Fig. 023

and sought more abstract forms of expression, using larger spaces to its performances.

Later on, at the beginning of the 20th century, Free dance was created by Isadora Duncan. Graduated in classical technique, she did not surrender to artificial and traditional principles from the classic, and inspired through the observations of the elements of nature – birds, waves (Fig.22) and even tree branches (Fig. 23). Those movements were fast, smooth and brought some value to space exploration (RANGEL, 2002).

Modern Dance had as one of its precursors the opera singer Franlois Delsarte, a Frenchman born in 1811. Due to the loss of speech at the age of 23, he had his career interrupted and developed an interest in the science of anatomy and the relationship between voice and gestures. Through the observations of madmen, drunks and dying in hospitals, he elaborated a technique of corporal expression with the objective of improving the performance of scenic artists. This technique characterized by movements of contraction and relaxation that translate an energy originated in the umbilical region connected to a respiratory work for better mastery and execution. The movements made with the trunk, arms and legs predict the suffering and the interior being of men (PORTINARI, 1989; ANGEL, 2002).

As mentioned by Godoy in the late twentieth century, after modern dance, Contemporary Dance came around emerging in the 60's and reaching up to the last decades. It brought new possibilities of movements and enabled the inclusion of all other techniques, which through any type of movement, whether technical or not, seeks to express, report, criticize or reflect on current issues and trends in our society. In this type of dance, fluidity expresses itself through the exploration of infinite possibilities of space and by the variation of technical and free movements, detached from rules, which refer to spontaneity and naturalness (RANGEL, 2002).

Another dance that emerged was Contact Improvisation, a dance type that came after contemporary dance in the United States by Steve Paxton in the 70s. He is a dancer, Olympic and Aikido gymnastics practitioner. Considered one of the living myths of dance, its research element was improvisation in dance and how this component could facilitate interaction between bodies, physical reactions and how to lead the egalitarian participation of people in a group, without arbitrarily employing social hierarchy. He wanted to develop a new kind of social organization, not dictatorial, not excluding. He idealized that dancing happened by itself and believed that any body could dance. The contactors, as they were called, moved together, rolling over each other, shifting the weight from one part of the body to another, from one body to the other, producing a fluid movement using the various levels of exploration (LEITE, 2005; VINHAS, 2007).

One of the characteristics of this modality is that the movement results from improvisation (HASELBACH, 1989 *apud* KRISCHKE, 2004) and improvising means doing something under certain conditions, not previously planned, adapting to difficulties (for example the object, which in dancing it would be the bodies). For the existence of improvisation, it is necessary to have spontaneity, or there will be no improvisation. With this, Contact Improvisation provokes and reacts to situations resulting from touching sensations and weight transfer, thus inventing solutions at the very moment when the dance happens.

Suggested Readings:

História da Dança, Portinari, M.B. ed. Nova Fronteira, 1989.

Dança Improvisação uma Relação a Ser Trilhada com o Lúdico, Krischke, A. M. Artigo Motricidade, 2004.

Contato Improvisação um Dialogo em Dança, Leite, F.H.C, Artigo Movimento, 2005.

CHAPTER 4

SAMIBALL METHOD®: CAPOEIRA AS A 3.RD SOURCE OF INSPIRATION

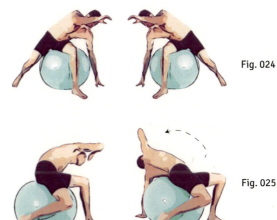

Fig. 024

Fig. 025

Through some practices and observations of martial arts such as capoeira, full contact and jiu-jitsu in my adolescence and adulthood, I adapted some martial arts moves to the ball aiming at taking new practices to my experiments. Hence, to make practice more interactive between Augusto (my training partner) and me, I adapted the movements to the ball better and better, having the basic movement of Gingar from capoeira as the pioneer movement (Fig. 24). From this movement on, I developed sequences that are more advanced.

49

Fig. 026

Fig. 027

As we were improving, I was creating and adapting new capoeira and full contact strokes on the ball. One day we went to the beach with the balls, we chose a place with some grass and I began to transmit some of my Capoeira adapted movements, more specifically the Dodge, the Blessing (Fig.26), the Aú (Fig.27), the Hammer (Fig.28) and the Sweep (Fig.29). With practice, we were already improvising a game of capoeira, without even realizing it, until a gentleman approached and said: "it's a capoeira on the ball, that's different!". Then I realized that the capoeira was there, being part of us, and that through his interpretation, that gentleman was able to visualize capoeira without having any type of identification such as white clothes, berimbau, music or rolling, for except our movements. My idea was born from that gentleman's imagination.

Fig. 028

Fig. 029

The connection between capoeira and Samiball is the resemblance of some movements, in which the practitioner is able to play capoeira, either slowly or quickly depending on the type of music played and whose objective is to unbalance the opponent from the ball and not to hurt or beat. With the use of the Swiss ball, people decrease the weight loaded on extremities, facilitating weight transfer between hands and feet, however they will need more balance for the accomplishment of the movements. As the ball is an unstable object with no steady base will naturally require more postural reactions (straightening, balancing and rectification reaction) from the individual.

I created the Gingando na Bola project some years later, as an initiative of my undergraduate thesis and the goal was to make practice more interactive among people. From that, I received new invitations for artistic presentations in a mix of capoeira and fighting. I was even invited to minister a course and present myself at the Capoeira Festival of Curitiba / Paraná in 2012 (Fig. 30 and 31).

The next topic is a brief review of Capoeira so that the reader can understand that some characteristics of capoeira in Samiball have served as a third source of inspiration.

Fig. 030   Fig. 031

4.1. CAPOEIRA

Capoeira was created out of the necessity by oppressed black people to get rid of their white oppressors as they did not possess enough weapons; and they realized that their own body could be a means of defense (BULAMAQUI, 1928 *apud* SILVA, 1993). They proved to be superior while fighting for agility, courage, cold-bloodedness and cunning, thus imitating movements of animals such as cats, monkeys (Fig. 32), horses, oxen, birds, snakes and structures of the manifestations brought from Africa (AREIAS, 1983 *apud* FREITAS, 1997).

Fig. 032

However, it is known that capoeira can be appreciated as history, philosophy of life, feelings of Brazilianness, music, dance, love and poetry, as it is characterized as a rich artistic expression which combines fight and dance using musical instruments like berimbau, tambourine and atabaque. (FRIGERIO, 1989). It can not be said in words, but in gestures and expression. In it a whole set of characteristic movements are present and, in this set of gestures and expressions, one must go beyond the mechanical fulfillment of the ritual to avoid a fragmentation, since in capoeira one has the sphere of the objective and the subjective, of the movement and of the meaning of it (Castro, 2003 *apud* D'Agostini, 2004). In capoeira, a constant corporal conversation happens among the players, all tuned in the game. The game composes a space in which one body speaks to another, from the relations established in the game and manifested in a language of its own, depending on the life history of each one. When a capoeirista crouches at the foot of the berimbau to start the game, there is no previous combination of the movements about to be performed, but rather a process of discovery based on what each one performs during the game (D'AGOSTINI, 2004).

We must emphasize that Capoeira plays "with" the other and not "against" the other. Practioners usually talk about "playing" capoeira and not "fighting" capoeira. In addition, since it is a game, it is necessary that the man plays as a child. (HUIZINGA, 1996, *apud* KRISCHKE, 2004). In this way, capoeira can be identified as play and/or looseness performed in wheels, (D'AGOSTINI, 2004), thus ensuring its connection to ludic aspects.

Regarding the practice itself, it is executed and practiced in an empirical, intuitive way, in which participants do not realize and create social, physical and spiritual results that contribute to formatting the human element (SENNA, 1980).

Capoeristas meet during wheels to play, have fun and go lazy. Traditionally a circle of about five meters in diameter is formed where all the participants can be seated or standing, depending on the traditions of each style, group or play of the berimbau, however these wheels are not limited to this physical space and generally begins with an "Iê" from the Master who is conducting the ritual. (VIEIRA, 1998; D'AGOSTINI, 2004).

The capoeira wheel is a field of mandinga, it is an astral field and it is a space of energy. The mandinga is the malice that during the course of the game, the player undoes a situation when his partner comes, an unexpected blow is applied and the other capoerista cannot react. One partner cheats the other in the game (CASTRO, 2003 *apud* D'AGOSTINI, 2004). In this game, it takes a lot of trickery and malice to know how to hide the moves and catch the other in a trap pretending to be distracted so that the opponent thinks this is his opportunity to attack. Worried about the action of attacking, the capoeirista is inattentive in his defense being able to be caught. This idea should not be confused as a retribution of a violent act or to be victorious, but pretending to be distracted and cheat the partner in his initiative of aggression (D'AGOSTINI, 2004).

The basic movement of capoeira is the Gingar. This movement serves for all other movements and consists of a rhythmic body swing that can be standardized or customized depending on each group of capoeira. Other movements of the capoeira are the sweeping, raytail, the head blow, the half-moon, the aú, the squatting, the blessing, the backward displacement, the negative open, the negative closed, the hammer, the role, the armed, the front scissor, the batflight and others.

Suggested Readings:

O Que é Capoeira, Areias, A. Ed. Brasiliense, 1983.

Capoeira, Arte Marcial Brasileira, Senna, C. Cadernos de cultura, 1980.

Capoeira do Engenho à Universidade, Cepesup 1993.

O Jogo de Capoeira: Cultura Popular no Brasil, Vieira, L.R. Ed. Sprint, 1998.

CHAPTER 5

SAMIBALL METHOD®: THE INFLUENCE OF PHYSIOTHERAPY

In 2006, I left the Physical Education course (Licenciature) and went to the Physical Therapy course, where I obtained specific knowledge about the human body through subjects such as Anatomy, Kinesiology, Biomechanics, Kinesiotherapy, Therapeutic Exercises, among others. As a teenager, I had experiences in paintings and drawings, so I took the opportunity to draw several bones, ligaments and muscles and this helped me to understand the theoretical basis of the method.

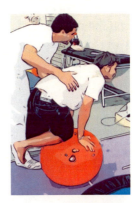

Fig. 033

When I began studying the practical disciplines of physical therapy, I had the opportunity to work with patients with different pathologies and sequels, such as asthma, cystic fibrosis, burns, amputees (Fig.33), low back pain and fibromyalgia. After this, I received some invitations, to talk about the method during my period involved with physical therapy (Fig.34).

Fig. 034

Physiotherapy is an applied science whose study object is the human movement, in all its forms of expression and potentialities, both in its pathological alterations and in its psychic and organic repercussions, in order to preserve, maintain and develop or restore the integrity of an organ, system, or function (Resolution COFFITO - 80, May 21, 1987).

It was in the last semester that I understood more clearly that I could introduce some movements in physiotherapy, since it is based on Anatomy, Kinesiology and Biomechanics and offer various forms of treatment such as thermotherapy, electrotherapy, phototherapy and kinesiotherapy.

Therefore, the method had the influence of physiotherapy and, because it fits within one of its modalities, the kinesiotherapy, its methodology has a theoretical basis through the knowledge and principles of kinesiology.

This is why that the aforementioned contents were inserted in the book through brief bibliographical reviews so that readers can understand and briefly visualize some concepts and nomenclatures. This may help the understanding of the exercises contained in this book.

5.1. KINESIOLOGY

Kinesiology refers to the study of human movement and was developed from the enchantment of human beings with animal movements, bringing up innumerable questions: How do the fish swim? (Fig. 35). How do birds fly? (Fig. 36) How does a person walk?. From the search for answers to these questions, the science of movement evolved, combined with theories and principles of anatomy, psychology, anthropology and mechanics (SMITH, 1997).

Fig. 035

In 1887, Muybridge used 48 photographic cameras and published the most remarkable photographs of humans while walking, running, jumping, climbing and lifting, as well as the marching of more than 30 animals and the flight of birds; totaling 8,000 photos (MUYBRIDGE, 1957 *apud* SMITH, 1997).

Fig. 036

The analysis of movements depends on a correct description of the joint movements that constitute each pattern of movement. The understanding of the movements in relation to the plane and the axis are of great importance for all professionals who work directly or indirectly with the movement. Doctors, physiotherapists, physical educators, sports coaches, athletic trainers, choreographers, dancers and other health professionals as they compose activities programs and have a better comprehension about body parts (BRITO, 2003).

The mechanics applied to the living human body is called biomechanics and has kinematics as one of its research elements. According to (AMPERO, ANDRE, 1775-1836, PINHEIRO 1992 *apud* D'AGOSTINO, 2004), kinematics is a term used to designate the part of the mechanics related to movements, with no consideration to the forces that produce them or the mass of the bodies in movement. It is the study of characteristics of the movement such as velocity and acceleration and related to a conventional frame and the decomposition of movements (SMITH, 1997).

The mechanics can be divided into static or dynamic.

- Static: the body is at rest or in uniform motion.
- Dynamics: the body is in acceleration or deceleration.

MOTION PLANS

All body actions generate movements and are perpendicular to movement. By convention, the articular movements are defined in relation to the anatomical position: erect body with united feet, upper limbs on the side of the body and the palms of the hand forward (RASCH, 1991).

To study the various joints of the body and analyze their movements, it is convenient to characterize them according to specific planes of motion. The plane of motion can be defined as an imaginary two-dimensional surface through which a limb or segment of the body is moved (THOMPSON, 1997).

There are four specific planes of motion according to which the various joint movements are classified. Although each specific joint movement begins in one of the planes of movement, our movements do not normally occur fully in one of the specific planes, but they occur as a conjugation of movements of more than one plane (THOMPSON, 1997).

The ball explored in this book presents a unique feature. According to Morais 1989 *apud* CASSOL, 2003 the ball works on all three planes due to its rounded shape making it a mobile, challenging object, making it possible to roll on flat surfaces. Due to this variety of directions that is possible to the ball, the individual moves on all planes.

Planes of Motion and Axes of Rotation

TABLE 1.1. PLANES AND AXES

Planes	Axes
Sagittal (median)	Lateral
Frontal (coronal)	Anteroposterior
Transversal (horizontal)	Vertical

FONTE: THOMPSON, 2002.

Planes and Axes

Planes: (sagittal - frontal - transverse – oblique)

SAGITTAL: this plane divides the body into the median line on the right side and the left side (Fig. 37). It is also named as anteroposterior plane. The movements performed in this plane are: flexion, extension, anteversion, retroversion, plantar flexion, dorsal flexion, elevation and scapular depression.

FRONTAL: divide the body from front to back represented by the (Fig. 38). Also called the coronal plane, the movements performed in this plane are: adduction, abduction, lateral flexion, inversion and eversion.

TRANSVERSE: this plane divides the body into the upper and the lower half (Fig. 37). It is also called horizontal plane. The movements performed in this plane are: external rotation, internal rotation, rotation to the right, rotation to the left, pronation and supination.

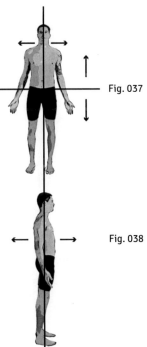

Fig. 037

Fig. 038

OBLIQUE: this plan is the sum of more than one plane. Most of the movements of the body are performed in this plane, because we perform a set of movements with certain complexity daily.

AXES: these imaginary lines are perpendicular to the planes on which the motion happens.

Gravity Center

It is the point of a solid body in which the sum of all moments due to weight is zero. It corresponds to the mass center. Theoretically, the center of gravity is determined by integral calculus and experimentally, by suspension of the body. That is, it is where the force of gravity acts. Since the center of mass is the point on which the mass is evenly distributed, it must also be the point of equilibrium of the body; therefore, the center of mass can be defined as the point on which the sum of the torques equals zero (HAMILL & KNUTZEN, 1999 *apud* D'AGOSTINI, 2004 p.23).

Although there is no anatomical center of gravity, its position will depend on the arrangement of the body segments and the changes that occur in the movement. It is known that the center of gravity of an adult human being in a static orthostatic position is slightly anterior to the second sacral vertebra (FRIZ, 2002; SMITH, 1997).

Balance

Fig. 039

Derived from the Latin word that means to balance. Its concept is exactly the result from the sum of the forces that is equal to zero. That is, it is the capacity that a human being has in maintaining its center of gravity on a support basis. The balance can be divided into stable and unstable. The stable refers to the return of the center of gravity to its previous position when it was slightly disturbed. The unstable is when the center of gravity goes to a new position at the moment of returning (SMITH Et all 1997; HALL, 2001). An example for balance is illustrated in figure 39.

The ball, the base instrument of the method and study object in this book, is one of the objects often used to work on the equilibrium of someone, as it provides an unstable surface in the performance of exercises.

Basis of support

Consists of the area that includes the outermost limits of the body in contact with the surface of the support (HALL, 2001 p.527).

The higher the support basis, the lower the requested balance, but if you have lower support basis, the greater the balance.

When transferred to the Swiss ball, the support basis will change according to the amount of air present in the ball. The fuller it is (Fig. 40), the smaller the support basis become and consequently the smaller the surface of contact of the ball with the ground necessitating a better balance. The less inflated the ball is (Fig. 41) the greater the support base and the contact surface of the ball with the ground, requiring less balance.

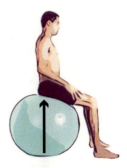

Fig. 040

The next content refers to Arthrology, and since it is a subject of great importance for body movement, a brief review of it was inserted in order to facilitate to the reader an understanding about the articular movements.

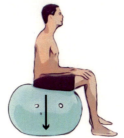

Fig. 041

5.2. ARTHROLOGY

It is defined as the study of joints (*arthros* = articulation + *logos* = study). The word articulation comes from the Latin *articulatione*, and according to the Aurélio Dictionary [3. Anat.] it is an organic device through which two or more bones remain in contact (Fig.42).

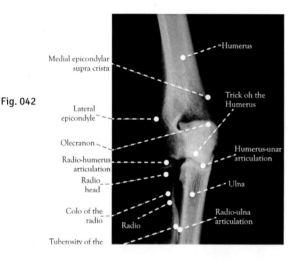

Fig. 042

Articulation of the elbow
AP view

A joint is used to connect and hold attached parts of a structure. In the body, the articulated structures are the bones. The joints illustrate the strong relationship between structures and function. The type of joint is directly related to its function or vice versa. The joints that cause stability or static sustainability differ from those that promote flexibility. In the body, structures such as the shape of bones and the way bones fit the joints determine the function of the joint. The joints can be classified into three types: synarthrosis, amphiarthrosis and synovial (FRITZ, 2002).

Classification of joints

- Synarthrosis: no joint movement.

- Amphiarthrosis: little joint movement.

- Synovial: major joint movement.

Fig. 043

On this book, we will discuss the diarthrosis-type joint as it is the most important one for our study. The Fig. 43 show points of some sinoval joints. Examples: Shoulder, elbow, handle, hip, knee and ankle.

The synovial joints are the most common, found in most joints and characterized as movable. By freedom of movement they can also be called diarthroses (diarthrosis = mobile joint). It is called a synovial joint because it contains a lubricating substance called synovial fluid coated by a synovial membrane or capsule. The synovial joints have peculiar characteristics: articular cartilage, joint capsule, synovial membrane and synovium (MIRANDA, 2006).

In these joints the surfaces of the bones are protected by a cartilage, characterized by very resistant fibrous tissue that covers the area where the bones meet. These are inside a joint capsule (GRAY, 1998).

There are six types of synovial joints that are grouped into: uniaxial (moves on only one axis), biaxial (allows movement on two axes) and triaxial (moves in several axes).

TYPES

- Uniaxial - movement only occurs on one of the body's planes. The two types of joints are in hinge (elbow) and pivot.

Articulation of the elbow
Profile view

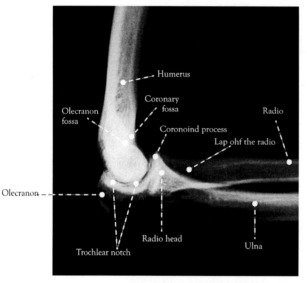

Fig. 044

KNEE JOINT
AP view

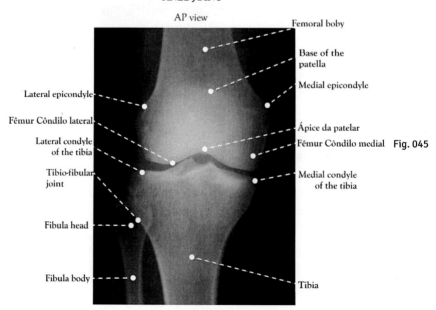

Fig. 045

Hinged joint allows you to perform extension and flexion movement. As examples we have the flexion and extension movements of the elbow and knee, respectively (Fig. 44 and 45, Profile View and AP View) respectively, and the interphalangeal. (FRITZ,2002).

The pivot joint allows you to perform the rotational movement. As examples we have the articulation between the first and second cervical vertebra and the joint at the proximal ends of the radius and ulna (Fig. 44) (HALL, 2001).

- Biaxial - movement occurs in two planes of the body. The two types of joints are condyloid and saddle.

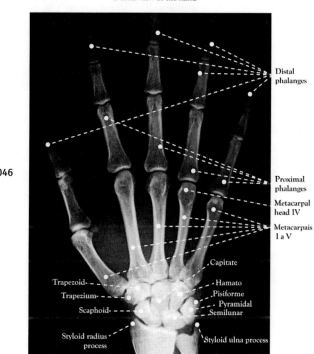

Fig. 046

The condyloid joint allows movement in two planes in this type of joint are flexion, extension, abduction and adduction. Some joints also perform rotation, in the case of the knee. As an example of condyloid are the wrist joints (Fig. 46 Dorsal view of the hand), the metacarpophalangeal, metatarsophalangeal, and atlantoccipital (FRITZ, 2002; HALL, 2009).

The saddle joint has a concavity in one joint and a convexity in the other joint. It allows movements of flexion, extension, abduction, and adduction. Examples of this joint are sternoclavicular, carpometacarpal, ankle joint (Fig. 47 profile view), among others.

ARTICULATION OF THE ANKLE

Profile view

Fig. 047

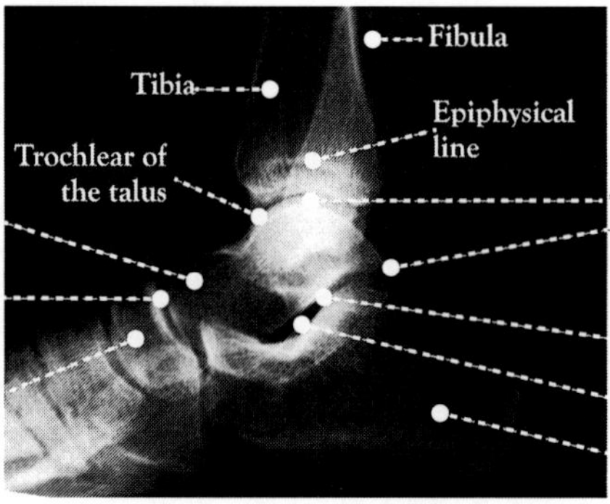

Labels: Fibula, Tibia, Epiphysical line, Taloctrual joint, Trochlear of the talus, Lap of the talus, Talocalcaneonavicular joint, Navicular, Posterior process of the talus, Subtalar joint, Breast of the talus, Heel

- Triaxial - movement occurs in three planes of the body or in the oblique plane, making a wide movement. The two types of joints are ball or socket and sliding.

The ball or socket joint is represented by the hip and shoulder joint (Fig. 48 and 49) where it performs extension, flexion, internal rotation, external rotation, adduction, abduction and circumduction movements (FRIZT, 2002).

The sliding joint is represented by the sacroiliac, tibiofibular, acromioclavicular joints and between the vertebral arches that allows sliding movements between two or more bones.

SHOULDER JOINT
AP view

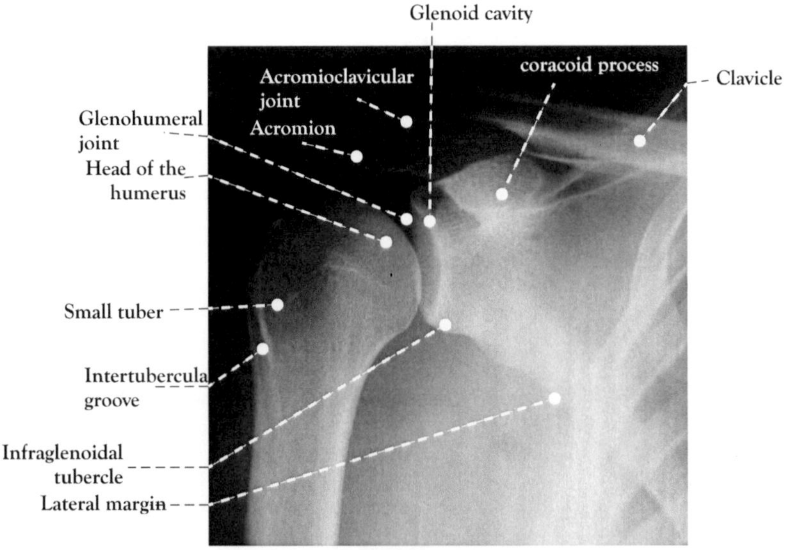

Fig. 048

HIP JOINT
AP view in orthostatic position

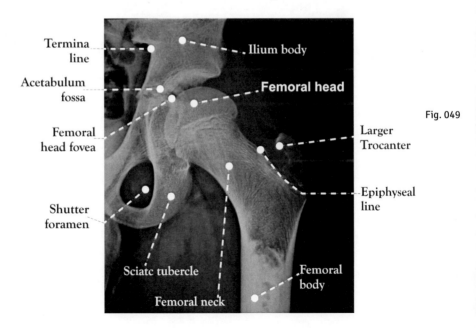

Fig. 049

SPINE

An example of the articular movements of the spine (Fig. 50) in the posturas on the ball and the behavior of the structures (Ligaments (Fig. 59), intervertebral disc and nucleus pulposus) in the movements.

FLEXION

VERTEBRAS IN FLEXION

Fig. 051

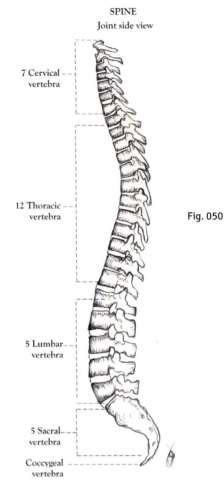

Fig. 050

Fig. 052

Flexion (Fig. 51 and 52): during bending of the spine, the intervertebral disc is compressed anteriorly and tensioned posteriorly and the nucleus pulposus posteriorly displaced. There is a tension of the posterior ligaments (interspinal ligament, supraspinatus ligament, intertransversal ligament, posterior vertebral ligament, yellow ligament and interapophyseal joint capsule) and the anterior ligament undergoes compression (KAPANJI, 2000).

EXTENSION

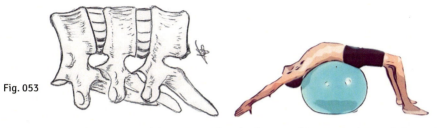

Fig. 053　　　　　　　　　　　　　　　　　　Fig. 054

Extension (Fig. 53 and 54): during the extension of the spine the intervertebral disc sharpens in the posterior part and widens in the anterior part and the nucleus pulposus moves anteriorly. The posterior ligaments undergo compression (interosseous ligament, intertranverse ligament, supraspinatus ligament, posterior longitudinal ligament, yellow ligament and capsule of interapophysial joints) whereas the anterior ligament is tensioned (anterior longitudinal ligament) (KAPANJI, 2000).

LATERAL FLEXION

VERTEBRAS IN LATERAL FLEXION

Fig. 055　　　　　　　　　　　　　　　　　　Fig. 056

Lateral flexion (Fig.55 and 56): during lateral flexion of the spine the intervertebral disc and the nucleus pulposus moves to the side of the convexity. The intervertebral ligament on the side of the convexity undergoes tension and compression on the side of the concavity. On the convex side the articulated apophysis of the superior vertebra undergoes a rise while the one on the side of the concavity undergoes a depression, simultaneously, a distension of the yellow ligaments and the articular capsule of the apophysis on the side of the concavity and a tension is given to the same elements of the convex side. (KAPANJI, 2000).

ROTATION

VERTEBRAS IN ROTATION

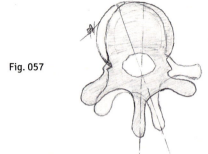
Fig. 057

Fig. 058

Rotation (Fig.57 and 58): During the rotation movement, the upper vertebral body rotates relative to the lower vertebral body, a shear between the two vertebrae occurring (KAPANJI, 2000).

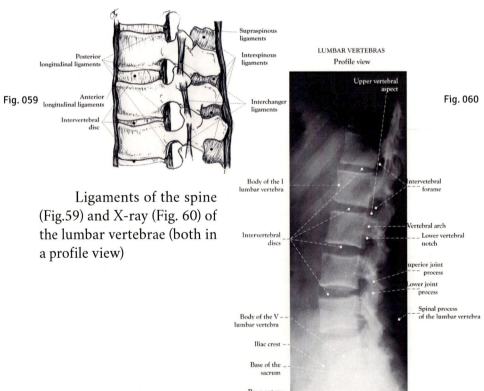

Fig. 059

Fig. 060

Ligaments of the spine (Fig.59) and X-ray (Fig. 60) of the lumbar vertebrae (both in a profile view)

70 SAMMIR VIEIRA MELO

MOVEMENTS OF SYNOVIAL JOINTS

1. FLEXION: decreased angle between two bones.

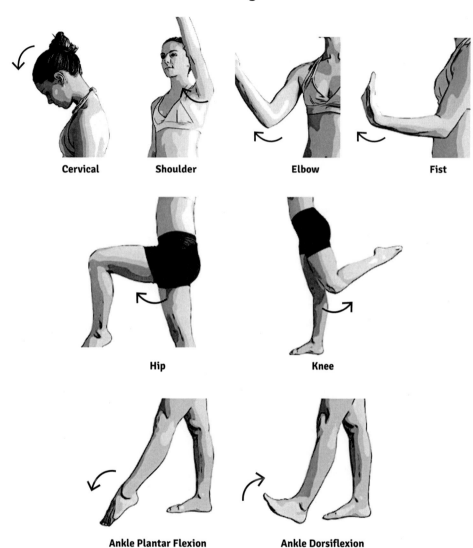

Cervical — Shoulder — Elbow — Fist

Hip — Knee

Ankle Plantar Flexion — Ankle Dorsiflexion

2. EXTENSION: increased angle between two bones.

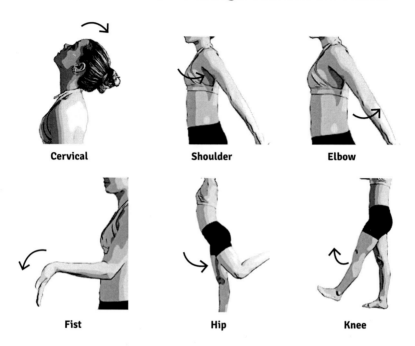

3. ABDUCTION: movement where the bone moves away from the median line.

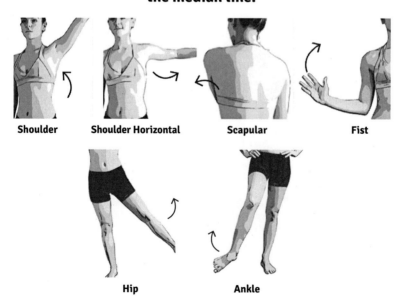

4. ADDUCTION: movement where the bone approaches the midline.

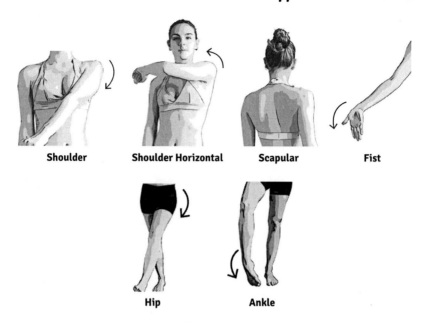

Shoulder   Shoulder Horizontal   Scapular   Fist

Hip   Ankle

5. ROTATION: when a bone moves around an axis.

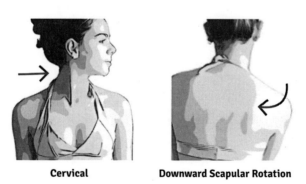

Cervical   Downward Scapular Rotation

6. SUPINATION: movement where the radius and ulna lie parallel to one another. The palm of the hand comes back up.

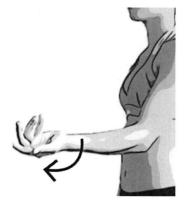

Supination

7. PRONATION: movement where the radius and ulna intersect and are not parallel to each other. Hand palm facing down.

Pronation

8. EVERSION: movement in which the sole of the foot stays out.

Eversion

9. INVERSION: movement in which the sole of the foot is inward.

Inversion

10. ELEVATION: scapular upward movemen. DEPRESSION: scapular downward movement.

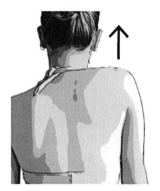
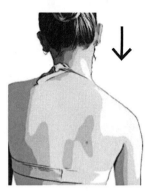

ARTICULAR ANALYSIS OF THE SAMIBALL MOVEMENTS

Fig. 061

POSTURE: twist.

SUPPORT BASE: one hand, one foot and the ball.

LEVEL: advanced.

ARTICULAR POSITIONS:
Column: rotation to the right; **Shoulders**: bilateral horizontal abduction; **Elbows**: bilateral extension; **Fists**: extension of left, neutral of right; **Hips**: right flexion, Left extension; **Knees**: flexion of the right, extension of the left; **Ankles**: neutral position.

Fig. 062

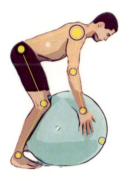

POSTURE: kneeling on the ball.

SUPPORT BASE: the feet and the ball.

LEVEL: basic.

ARTICULAR POSITIONS:
Column: neutral position; **Shoulders**: bilateral flexion; **Elbows**: bilateral slight flexion; **Handles**: slight bilateral extension; **Hips**: bilateral flexion; **Knees**: bilateral flexion; **Ankles**: bilateral dorsiflexion.

Fig. 063

POSTURE: gingar

SUPPORT BASE: the feet, one hand and the ball

LEVEL: moderate

ARTICULAR POSITIONS:
Column: slight right lateral flexion; **Shoulders**: left flexion, abduction horizontal of the law; **Elbows**: flexion of the left and slight flexion of the right; **Handles**: bilateral neutral position; **Hips**: flexion of the right and abduction of the left; **Knees**: flexion of the right and extension of the left; **Ankles**: position neutral of the right and inversion of the left.

Fig. 064

POSTURE: dodge

SUPPORT BASE: the feet, one hand and the ball

LEVEL: basic

ARTICULAR POSITIONS:
Column: cxtension position with slight rotation and lateral flexion; **Shoulders**: bilateral abduction; **Elbows**: extension of the left and flexion of the right; **Fists**: left extension (solo); **Hips**: left flexion and right extension; **Knees**: bilateral flexion; **Ankles**: right plantar flexion and slight left dorsiflexion.

Fig. 065

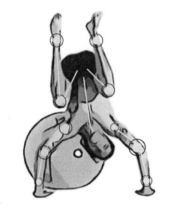

POSTURE: handstand

SUPPORT BASE: hands and ball

LEVEL: advanced

ARTICULAR POSITIONS:
Column: cervical: lateral, thoracic and lumbar flexion: flexion; **Shoulders:** bilateral abduction; **Elbows:** bilateral flexion; **Fists:** bilateral extension; **Hips:** bilateral flexion; **Knees:** bilateral flexion; **Ankles:** slight bilateral plantar flexion.

Fig. 066

POSITION: snail in dorsal decubitus.

SUPPORT BASE: hands and ball

LEVEL: advanced

ARTICULAR POSITIONS:
Column: flexion; **Shoulders:** bilateral hyperextension; **Elbows:** bilateral extension; **Fists:** bilateral extension; **Hips:** bilateral flexion; **Knees:** bilateral flexion; **Ankles:** slight bilateral plantar flexion.

Fig. 067

POSTURE: pendulum on the wall

SUPPORT BASE: the ball on the ground, feet on the wall;

LEVEL: moderate;

ARTICULAR POSITIONS:
Column: slight flexion with rotation; **Shoulders**: bilateral abduction; **Elbows**: bilateral flexion; **Handles**: lightweight bilateral flexion; **Hips**: flexion of the right and flexion with abduction of the left; **Knees**: flexion of the right and extension of the left; **Ankles**: slight dorsal flexion of the right and slight plantar flexion with inversion of the left.

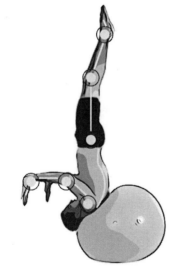

Fig. 068

POSTURE: candle on the wall.

SUPPORT BASE: hands on the wall and ball on the ground

LEVEL: advanced

ARTICULAR POSITIONS:
Column: flexion cervical; neutral position; **Shoulders**: bilateral flexion with slight abduction; **Elbows**: bilateral flexion; **Fists**: bilateral extension; **Hips**: bilateral extension; **Knees**: bilateral extension; **Ankles**: bilateral plantar flexion

Fig. 069

POSTURE: flexion

SUPPORT BASE: rail of the board and the ball

LEVEL: basic

ARTICULAR POSITIONS:
Column: flexion; **Shoulders**: bilateral flexion; **Elbows**: extension and bilateral pronation; **Handles**: slight bilateral extension; **Hips**: bilateral flexion; **Knees**: bilateral extension; **Ankles**: bilateral dorsiflexion

Fig. 070

POSTURE: grabbing edge.

SUPPORT BASE: the ball

LEVEL: advanced

ARTICULAR POSITIONS:
Column: flexion; **Shoulders**: bilateral flexion; **Elbows**: bilateral extension; **Fists**: bilateral extension; **Hips**: bilateral maximal flexion; **Knees**: bilateral flexion; **Ankles**: bilateral dorsal flexion

Fig. 071

POSTURE: grab rail

SUPPORT BASE: the ball, the feet and one of the knees (board)

LEVEL: basic

ARTICULAR POSITIONS:
Column: light bending; **Shoulders**: neutral position of right and slight abduction of left; **Elbows**: slight bilateral flexion; **Fists**: slight bilateral extension; **Hips**: bilateral flexion; **Knees**: bilateral flexion with external rotation of the right and internal rotation of the left; **Ankles**: slight left dorsiflexion, right eversion.

Fig. 072

POSTURA: air grab rail

SUPPORT BASE: the ball, one hand

LEVEL: advanced

ARTICULAR POSITIONS:
Column: slight flexion, lateral flexion; **Shoulders**: flexion of the left and horizontal abduction of the right; **Elbows**: flexion of the right and extension of the left; **Fists**: extension of the right and neutral of the left; **Hips**: bilateral flexion with slight left abduction; **Knees**: flexion with external rotation of the right and extension of the left; **Ankles**: slight dorsal flexion of the left, eversion of the right.

Fig. 073

POSTURE: aerial with grab rail and no hand on the ball;

SUPPORT BASE: the ball

LEVEL: Advanced

ARTICULAR POSITIONS:
Column: flexion; **Shoulders:** left hyperextension and right flexion; **Elbows:** extension with bilateral supination; **Fists:** slight bilateral extension; **Hips:** bilateral flexion; **Knees:** bilateral flexion; **Ankles:** bilateral dorsiflexion

Fig. 074

POSTURE: cut back

SUPPORT BASE: the ball and board

LEVEL: basic

ARTICULAR POSITIONS:
Column: rotation; **Shoulders:** hyperextension of the right and flexion of the left; **Elbows:** bilateral flexion; **Fists:** slight bilateral extension; **Hips:** bilateral flexion; **Knees:** slight right flexion and flexion with left external rotation; **Ankles:** eversion of the left and inversion of the right

Next topic to be addressed will be Muscles, subject of great value for understanding the movements on the ball. The skeletal type muscles mentioned in the book are responsible for producing voluntary body movements and for this reason; a brief review was introduced to facilitate the reader's comprehension.

5.3 MUSCLES

All the physical functions of the body imply muscular activity. These functions include skeletal movements, contraction of the heart, contraction of blood vessels, peristalsis of the gut and many others (GUYTON, 1998).

The muscular system consists of the skeletal (Fig. 75, 76, 78, 79, 80, 81, 82 and 83), cardiac and smooth muscles, as well as the attached elements (tendons, fascia, aponeuroses, blood vessels and nerve fibers). Muscle tissue is responsible for the contraction and distension force of its cells, where the attached elements will form a system of levers to assist movement of the limbs and viscera. The human body is composed of approximately 40% skeletal muscle, which is primarily responsible for the conversion of chemical (potential) energy into kinetic energy (movement). The skeletal muscles are covered by a thin blade, the perimysium or fascia, which extends into the muscle as a septum of lesser thickness, the endomysium from which the smaller compartments are derived. These compartments are the fascicles and each one contains a number of fibers bound to the endomysium. (GUYTON, 1993).

On this book, we will briefly mention only the skeletal muscles because they are responsible for the voluntary and active movements performed with the ball.

TRUNK MUSCLES

Fig. 075

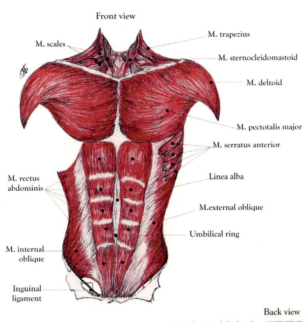

Fig. 076

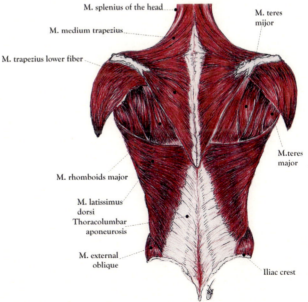

For the skeleton to perform a movement, some muscles need to perform certain contractions which are divided into isometric or static and isotonic or dynamic contractions, depending on the work performed.

The Isometric or static

It happens when tension develops within the muscle, but there is no perceptible change in joint angle or muscle length, and is also known as static contraction. The strength developed by the muscle is equal to the resistance (THOMPSON; FLOYD, 1997 p. 17). Contratcions and as an example we have Fig.77.

Fig. 077

The Isotonic or dynamic

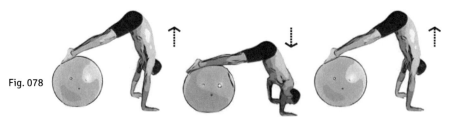
Fig. 078

It happens when tension develops in the muscle as it lengthens or shortens; is also known as dynamic contraction and can be classified as concentric or eccentric. The strength developed by the muscle is greater or less than the resistance (THOMAS; FLOYD, 2002. p.17). Example of isotonic contraction shown in fig Fig.78.

Contraction of the isotonic type Fig. 79, concentric and eccentric contractions are present. For example, the diaphragm muscle that works in this type of contraction. Fig. 79.

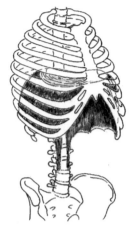

Fig. 079

Concentric

It is when the muscle exerts a tension and there is a decrease in its length and this applied force is against the gravity or against the resistance known as positive force THOMPONS; FLOYD, 2002).

Eccentric

It is when the muscle performs a tension and there is an increase in its length, that is, there is a stretching of it, making this applied force to be in favor of gravity or resistance. This tension is gradually decreased to control movement and is also known as negative contraction (HARRIS,2002).

ROLE OF MUSCLES

AGONIST: the muscle contracts concentrically and overcomes the resistance being the main muscle in the accomplishment of a movement. (THOMPONS; FLOYD, 2002).

ANTAGONIST: the muscle performs the opposite function to the agonist, resulting in the increase of its size, controlling the movement in an eccentric form, where the external force torque overcomes the muscular force torque.

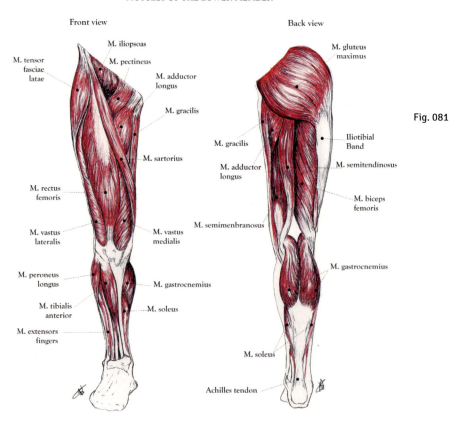

MUSCLES OF THE LOWER MEMBER

Fig. 080

Fig. 081

ACCESSORIES

These are muscles that indirectly work in the accomplishment of a movement and are divided in:

STABILIZERS: Muscles that stabilize a segment of the body so that another active muscle has a firm basis and can perform its function.

SYNERGISTS: it is the simultaneous interaction of all muscles actions involved in the movement.

NEUTRALIZERS: it is when the muscle comes into action with the goal of overriding the actions of the agonists.

The interaction of these various muscle roles is noted when performing exercises on the ball, due to be an unstable object without a fixed support basis, which requires an interaction between all these functions already discussed above.

REGARDING THE NUMBER OF ARTICULATION THAT CAN BE CROSSED.

Monoarticular – They are muscles in which their origin and insertion cross and act in only one joint.

Example: vastus medialis, vastus lateralis, vastus intermedius (Fig. 80), pectoralis major (Fig. 75 and Fig. 82), teres major, teres minor (Fig. 83) soleus (Fig. 80 and Fig.81) (NEUMANN, 2005).

Biarticular – They are muscles where their origin and insertion cross and act on two joints. Example: rectus femoris (Fig. 80), gastrocnemius (Fig. 81), triceps (Fig. 83), arm biceps (Fig. 82).

Multiarticular – The origin and insertion of the muscle cross and act on three or more joints. Examples: spine erector, splenius, trapezius (Fig. 76), rhomboids (Fig. 76) and others.

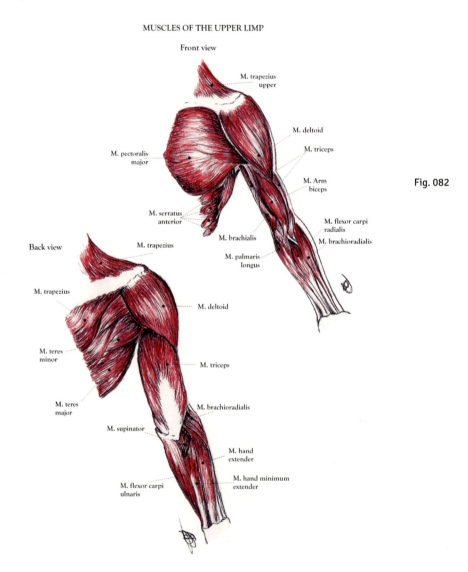

TYPES OF FIBERS

Cincerning the types of fibers, the muscles of the human body are composed by a mix of fast and slow muscle fibers. Rapidly reacting muscles are mainly composed of fast fibers. Conversely, muscles that respond slowly to the prolonged contraction stimulus are composed primarily of slow fibers.

Skeletal muscle fiber is classified according to the intensity and duration of the contraction it produces. Type I (slow contraction) muscle fibers produce low intensity contractions but as they use the aerobic energy system contractions can be maintained for a long period. As they take longer to show fatigue, these fibers predominate in postural muscles (for example, the erector spinae muscles and those in the quadriceps femoral group) Fig. 80. Type II muscle fibers (rapid contraction) primarily use the anaerobic energy system and produce high-intensity, short-term contractions. These fibers, capable of generating a large amount of force over a short period are predominant in muscle contractions. Type II fibers are subdivided into type II-B, which are fully anaerobic, and type II-A, having characteristics of type I and II fibers (STARKEY, 2001, p. 7).

NOMENCLATURE OF SKELETAL MUSCLES

Each muscle brings a nomenclature and most of the time this terminology says a lot about it. The nomenclature tends to follow some categories such as location, shape, division number or heads, fixations - origin / insertions, fiber directions and muscle size. An example is the anterior tibialis (Fig. 80) muscle and as the name indicates, it is located on the anterior surface of the tibia. The sternocleidomastoid (Fig. 75) joins the bones of the sternum, clavicle, and mastoid. Pectoralis major (Fig. 75 and Fig. 82) and minor indicate that one is larger than the other, although these two muscles are in the same area (LIPPER, 1996).

FUNCTIONAL CHARACTERISTICS OF MUSCLES

Muscles have specific properties such as contractility, elasticity, extensibility, and irritability. No body tissue incorporates all these properties in one.

Contractility is the muscle ability to contract or shorten thus producing a tension between the extremities. Elasticity is the ability to shrink or return to its initial resting size when the force is removed. Extensibility is the muscle's ability to stretch when a force is applied. Irritability is the ability of the muscle to respond to stimuli (LIPPER, 1996).

The next addressed topic brings a brief review of kinesiotherapy, whose purpose is to demonstrate to the reader how much the Samiball® Method can be used as a kinesiotherapy tool as it promotes movement as a form of treatment.

5.4 KINESIOTHERAPY

From 4000 BC to 395 AD, the priests employed body movement as a form of healing for some established and installed dysfunctions. At the end of the Middle Ages and at the beginning of the Renaissance, body beauty started to be more appreciated and in this same period, physical exercise was linked to physical beauty, thus generating a preoccupation with the body. As the human movement was being highly valued in Ancient Greece, the philosopher Aristotle (384 BC) already described the action of muscles and rehabilitation by movement and became the "Father of Kinesiology" (SANCHEZ, 1994; CRUZ, 2003).

In Chinese literature and since 2698 BC, Kinesiotherapy referred to the healing by movement and this involves the use of voluntary and repetitive body exercises as a treatment based on the knowledge of anatomy, physiology and biomechanics. This knowledge provides the patient a better and effective work of prevention, healing and rehabilitation (AMARO, 2001; CRUZ, 2003).

Such body exercises are classified as aesthetic, sporting and therapeutic. The latter maintain, correct and / or recover a regular function, i.e. restore a normal function and maintain well-being. Its main purpose is to maintain or develop the free movement for the function. Its effects are based on the development, restoration and maintenance of strength, resistance to fatigue, mobility and flexibility, relaxation, coordination and balance (KISNER & COLBY, 2005).

In Greece and Ancient Rome, the first studies were carried out using therapeutic exercises, but it was not until World War I that there was an increase in using this rehabilitation modality (CRUZ, 2003).

Today, these therapeutic exercises are used in physiotherapy and seek to achieve a better quality of life for the citizen, through the intervention of methodologies and techniques based on the therapeutic use of physical and chemical movements and phenomena, in the face of intercurrent dysfunctions (COFFITO 1969 *apud* CRUZ, 2003).

These therapeutic exercises are considered a central element in most physiotherapy care plans in order to improve function and reduce disability. Its indication is very careful, requiring a thorough evaluation to outline goals and strategies, and frequent reassessments aimed at updating the patient's progression as a consequence for corrections to the initial program until reaching the expected recovery potential (CRUZ, 2003).

Among the kinesiotherapy techniques, we can mention some types of therapeutic exercises such as free active exercises, assisted and passive actives. These can be performed in breathing exercises, stretching exercises (Fig.85), conditioning exercises (Fig. 86), coordination exercises, balancing exercises, and postural exercises. (Fig.84 and 87).

Fig. 084 Balance

Fig. 085 Stretching

Fig. 086 Coordination and Conditioning

Fig. 087 Postural

Physiotherapeutic treatment through kinesiotherapy may be favored using several resources from the mechanotherapy. Mechanotherapy is one of the physical therapy parts involving the use of mechanical procedures, devices, and equipment for the purpose of developing strength, endurance, improving range of motion, allowing traction or pressure, balancing forces, and mobilizing body segments besides monitoring procedures during therapy (DOMBOVY, 1986).

Such devices as a Swiss ball, rolls, Thera-Band elastic, dumbbells, Ling bar, orthostatic board, quadriceps board, Balkan frame, Bonet chair, leg press, stationary bike, treadmill, parallel bar, progressive ladder, ramp, balancing boards, trampoline, rocker, RPG table, Voldyne, triflo, flutter and peak flow are all available for physical therapy treatments. This book addressed only the first resource, the Swiss ball.

The next subject is the application of the Samiball Method in kinesiotherapy in order to demonstrate to the reader that the applied method had therapeutic intentions to develop, treat and work the physical capacities of students and patient.

CHAPTER 6

SAMIBALL METHOD®: APPLICATION IN KINESIOTHERAPY

It was in 2009 that I began to apply the SAMIBALL Method as a form of kinesiotherapy. I still was a Physiotherapy graduate student and concerned about the relationship of posture and the health of my parents (Fig.88, before, above and below below). I thought about teaching them some movements focused on postural work. And this was under the guidance and supervision of Prof. ª Dr. ª Rose. Therefore, I selected some movements and taught them to my parents. Afterwards, some friends showed some interest to learn as well since most of them are surfers. (Fig. 89).

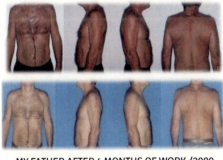

Fig. 088

MY FATHER AFTER 4 MONTHS OF WORK /2009

Fig. 089

Also in the same year, I had the opportunity to work and assist some mothers of patients in a university project, focusing on postural work (Fig. 90). I still worked with a patient who had her body burned (trunk, abdomen, thighs and arm) when she was a child. This patient used drugs to inhibit growth and reduce pain. At the University trainee period, I started the first sessions aiming at improving her mobility and flexibility of the trunk, especially in the regions affected by the scar. We performed an evaluation and applied the third finger test to the ground in order to measure the flexibility of the posterior chain. We had more than 30 sessions and got good results. I transferred this patient to Avosos to join the other patients of the Assistance House Aunt Ruth, an NGO (Fig. 91). I started the project "Gingando na bola" at this NGO, with the purpose of developing my Undergraduate Thesis (Fig.92 a/b).

This project was carried out at the Assistance House Aunt Ruth - Avosos (Volunteers Association for Oncology Services in Sergipe), and it started with cancer patients, sickle cell anemia and dermatological dysfunction, all clinically stable and under observation, the objective was improving the conditioning, flexibility, balance, motor coordination and we aimed at improving patients quality of life.

Under the guidance of Prof.[a] Rosemeire Dantas, patients were taken to a physical therapy evaluation pre-session where they answered a questionnaire about their quality of life, they took a six-minute treadmill test, postural and respiratory evaluation (using PeakFlow), flexibility test through the 3rd finger, goniometry, cirtometry, skinfolds and balance test.

As classes went by, I taught them a series of techniques ranging from yoga breathing exercises (pranayamas) and stretching exercises to the Samiball movements adapted to Capoeira. There was a whole process of monitoring, observing the evolution through the progression of the movements taught and reevaluations were carried out. The sessions were becoming more and more interactive among the patients to the point where we performed capoeira games based on the Samiball. These games were accompanied by music to facilitate the movements rhythm. From this action of the project Gingando na Bola, other invitations for presentations strated to happen. Therefore, we were present at the 20th Physiotherapy Week at a University (Fig.92a) and at the III Workshop on Combating Child and Adolescent Cancer (fig.92b).

Following the application of this project, I came to the conclusion that the Samiball® Method can fit into Kinesiotherapy. However, only patients who are compatible with their physical conditions can do so and the proposed activities have to be regular ones. The effort has to progress slowly and registered physiotherapists must monitor the appropriate measure for this physical effort. This project resulted in three scientific articles published in 2011. The abstracts are available at the following pages.

Fig. 090

Fig. 92a

Fig. 091

Fig. 92b

SCIENTIFIC PAPERS:

The Samiball® Method and its effects on the flexibility and expandability of burn victims: a case report

ABSTRACT

Objective: To evaluate the effects of the Samiball Method on the flexibility and expandability of burn victims. Case Report: Female patient, 18 years old, victim of thermal trauma due to incineration of the garments. It presents extensive scars on the anterior, lateral and posterior trunk, limiting movements and decreasing thoracic expansibility. The work was approved by the Ethics and Research Committee at Tiradentes University (SE) and developed at AVOSOS (Association of Volunteers at the Service of Oncology in Sergipe) for 30 sessions of 60 minutes, 3 times a week. 3rd finger-soil test, lumbar goniometry and thoracometry were performed. The physiotherapeutic protocol was divided into warming up, conditioning and relaxation. Results: In the first evaluation, the finger-soil test result was 18 cm; in the second one, the value went to 3 cm and in the last it reached 0 cm and the patient touched the 3rd finger-soil. In lumbar goniometry for flexion, the value went from 64° to 98°. For lumbar extension, it went from the initial 30° to 34° at the end. In right lateral flexion, it went from 14° before the treatment to 30° after it. At last, left lateral flexion was 20° at the beginning and 28° at the end. The axillary coefficient increased from 4.5 cm to 5.0 cm, while the xiphoid coefficient ranged from 4.0 cm to 5.0 cm, and the baseline, from 2.5 cm to 4.5 cm. Conclusion: The therapeutic proposal by the Samiball method was effective, increasing thoracic expandability and flexibility of the lumbar and the posterior chain.

Source: REVISTA BRASILEIRA DE QUEIMADURA. v. 10, p. 71-74, 2011.

The Samiball® Method and its effects on heart rate and performance of patients with Sickle Cell Anemia: a case report

ABSTRACT

Sickle cell anemia is a hereditary disease manifested by hypoxia, painful crises, fever and fatigue. The Samiball Method was developed by Sammir Vieira Melo, adapting movements of yoga, dance and capoeira to the Swiss ball. The aim of this study was to evaluate the effect of this method on heart rate and performance of patients with sickle cell anemia. This is a descriptive study of a case report type with two male patients aged 18 to 21, during 30 sessions of 60 minutes, 3 times a week. In the initial evaluation, a questionnaire was performed and then patients were evaluated through the six-minute walk test on the treadmill. During the test, HR and AP were measured as well as the level of dyspnea (Modified Borg Scale). The treatment was divided into warming up, conditioning and relaxation. The results were analyzed in Excel 2007 and showed that resting HR decreased from 95.5 bpm to 75 bpm after treatment. The Borg Scale went from moderate to very light and the speed increased from 5 km / h to 6.25 km / h. The average walking distance went from 450 m to 495 m. Sickle patients have poor performance in physical activities and this limits many professionals in prescribing exercises. The conclusion is that the Samiball Method promoted a decrease in post-treatment rest HR and an improvement in performance.

Keywords: Swiss Ball; Kinesiotherapy; Physical exercise.

Source: REVISTA BRASILEIRA DE PRESCRIÇÃO E FISIOLOGIA DO EXERCÍCIO, v. 5, p. 446-452, 2011.

CHAPTER 7

SAMIBALL METHOD®: THE INFLUENCE OF BOARDSPORTS - SURFING AND KITESURFING

After my graduation and as a registered physiotherapist, I created and applied the ball exercises to some friends and specifically for Surfing and Kitesurfing.

Fig. 093

My experience with these two sports comes from many years ago (Fig. 93 and 95) as I started surfing when I was only 13 years old. It was a sport that fascinated me and since the day I tried on I never stopped parcticing it. I believe that the connection with the ocean and nature attracted me more and more, although, in 1993, surfing had a bad reputation and was not accepted by society, including my family. This was no reason for me to give up and

Fig. 094

made me stronger to continue in a sport that encompasses many factors and elements of nature.

At first, surfing was a kind of fun and discovery pastime, practiced for the simple fact of sliding on the waves and being in contact with nature and friends. Gradually this sport became my way of life. As I have never been a competitive person, I surfed for simple pleasure. My focus was always surfing and working my body so that whenever I went surfing I could go further, be it in paddling, in performance, in strength or in balance. I believe this was one of the reasons for creating and developing some movements on the ball.

Fig. 095　　　　　　　　　　　　　　　　　　　　　　　　　　　Fig. 096

Nowadays, some health professionals are suggesting surfing as a form of therapy or physical activity because it involves multiple aspects to the human body. It ranges from the bodywork generated by surfing such as paddling or swimming, balance lying down and standing up on the board, combined movements of the trunk, legs and arms. It also provides a mental work by involving emotions and feelings such as fear, self-confidence and happiness, all connected to the sea and nature when practicing this sport.

Therefore, the influence of surfing in this Method was on my ability to work on ball exercises and bring some surfing movements to be adapted and simulated. These movements and postures are represented in figures 93, 94, 95, 96, 97, 98, 100 and 104. They improve some physical capacities like flexibility, balance, coordination, among others.

Fig. 097   Fig. 098

The other sport that had great influence in Samiball was kitesurfing. I started practicing the sport when I was 34 (Fig. 99) and this sport is relatively new when compared to surfing.

Fig. 099   Fig. 100

The equipment for kite practice involved inflatable kites. Today, the equipment also includes a bar, a harness and the board. There are two types of boards: the directional ones which are also called conventional boards and have the outline of common surfboards with some slight changes; and the bidirectional ones which are similar to wakeboards and can be thinner or thicker depending on the purpose of them.

I started kitesurfing because the city where I live suffers great influences from the winds. As a restless young man, I thought it would be a second option for ocean sports and therefore I got into it. As I was older, 34 years old, I saw in the ball a new training option to anticipate (Fig.101) and facilitate my kitesurf learning. After I started some practice with the ball and the board, I soon realized the similarity in some postures. (Fig.102 and 103).  Fig. 101

THE AWAKENING OF MOVEMENT WITH THE BALL - SAMIBALL® AND ITS RAMIFICATIONS

Fig. 102   Fig. 103

Through these experiences with these two sports, I adapted some movements through the use of the ball and a board. The board used for this new method creation was the kitesurfing one as it is smaller and it has footstraps. Hence, I was able to perform and combine some kitesurf and surf moves for the ball as a kind of simulation of the movements of those sports. Postures resemble kite and surf moves biomechanically and the objective is to enable a similar experience of postures on the ball. This out of the water practice works on muscle memory and joint positions and develop individuals' physical capacities.

Fig. 104

3 DIFFERENT POSTURES:

Flexion Posture **Extension Posture** **Balance**

Fig. 105 Fig. 106 Fig. 107

FOOT OUT OF THE STRAP (forward and backward) IN LATERAL DECUBITUS :

Fig. 108

CHAPTER 8

SAMIBALL® METHOD: CONCEPTS AND MATURATION

Through these experiences of working with the Swiss ball, whether in art form or health rehabilitation, prevention, training and sports, I started to give shape to the Samiball® method.

At first, I identified the four primary positions (Fig. 109 to 112). The Samiball Method offers four basic positions that were called **primary positions** because all other positions are derived from them.

1. Sitting:

The practitioner is seated (Fig. 109) on the ball, with the knees and hip flexed at a 90º angle. The spine is erect, arms along the body or abducted horizontally and elbows are flexed. Variation with one limb and knee extended (Fig. 155). The body part in contact with the ball is the ischium while the support basis are both feet and the ball.

Fig. 109

2. Back:

The practitioner has a straight or slightly bent spine in contact with the ball (thoracic and lumbar region). Knees fully flexed and hip flexed 90º, arms in neutral position. The body part in contact with the ball is the back and the support basis are both feet and the ball.

Fig. 110

3. Chest:

The practitioner keeps the chest area leaning against the ball, gluteus in contact with the leg posterior view on plantar flexion. Knees fully flexed, hip flexion at almost a 90º angle and slight trunk flexion. Arms and elbow extended or slight flexed, wrist extension resting the palm of the hand on the ground. There may be a variation with hip and knees extended (Fig. 185). The anterior trunk region is in contact with the ball and the support basis here is the ball, the leg anterior view when the knee is flexed or the feet when the knee is extended as well as the hands.

Fig. 111

4. Knee:

The practitioner leans the leg anterior view on the ball, with knees and hip flexed. Trunk slightly flexed to the shoulders, elbows and fists extended and hand palm on the ground as support. Cervical spine in extension or in bending for rest. There may be a variation with the hip and knees in extension (Fig. 202). Leg anterior view in contact with the Swiss ball and the support basis is the hands and the ball in the ground.

Fig. 112

8.1 THE PURPOSES OF THE METHOD

The method was initially created for performances and choreographies however, when I used it for health rehabilitation, prevention, training or sports I realized they developed and worked on balance, flexibility, coordination motor, postural alignment, physical conditioning and strength as well as improvement of mechanical ventilation, relaxation and body awareness.

After that, I fully understood that the method encompassed two different areas. Health as in rehabilitation, prevention, training and sports and Arts as in Dancing and Martial Arts. Since then, I have developed some theoretical foundations such as ramifications, basic principles and the stages.

8.2 RAMIFICATIONS OF THE SAMIBALL METHOD®

Samiball ramification in the health area happens as the method is composed of several conventional and exclusive body movements, from basic movements to most advanced ones, all performed actively and through voluntary muscular action, that is, with skeletal muscles contraction to produce movement. That is why Samiball Method can fit into kinesiotherapy (therapeutic) and physical activity (preventive and training). According to Carpersen, (1985) physical activity consists of any body movement produced by the skeletal musculature, resulting in energy expenditure above resting levels. Therefore, Samiball Method can be used as a physical exercise or physical preparation, provided that the exercises proposed are guided by a qualified professional and follow a planning.

As for the ramification linked to the Arts area, the Samiball method aims at artistic choreography performances through dancing in contact-improvisation and with capoeira (Fig.113c). On these, the use of the ball expresses an experiment, thinking or a feeling.

According to Valerio (2001), if the artist expresses himself, he is making Art. This is the reason why Art is an indirect way of transmitting, expressing, and materializing emotions in people. It is indirect because it differs from ordinary personal communication where we can express ourselves emotionally.

THE THREE RAMIFICATIONS OF THE SAMIBALL® METHOD:

1.st **Ramification** – (Fig. 113a) the first ramification or branch is the THERAPEUTIC Samiball that is based on kinesiotherapy and uses exercises in a therapeutic way. The aim is developing free movements for its function and it is recommended to people who present some type of impairment.

2.nd **Ramification** – (Fig. 113b) the second one is the PREVENTIVE / FUNCTIONAL Samiball and it uses exercises to preserve, prepare, and train the body for sports provided it follows a structured planning. It is recommended for those who do not present any type of impairment and aims at developing physical fitness.

2.rd **Ramification** – (Fig. 113c) the third is the Samiball ART and this modality encompasses and uses the two previous ones from above and aims at creating choreographies to be used in artistic performances.

Fig. 113a   Fig. 113b   Fig. 113c

8.3 BASIC PRINCIPLES

Four basic principles are present in the Samiball method. The 1st basic principle is Breathing. This is essential for the development of the 2nd principle, Concentration. From the interaction of the two first principles, there is the improvement of the third one, physical and mental balance. Such a balance extends the individual's perception to the four principle, body awareness.

These basic principles intertwine and form the five stages that compose the method.

8.4 STAGES

1.st STAGE

BREATHING: the first step of the method relies on breathing, composed of some basic breathing techniques taken from yoga and adapted to it. Involving corporal and mental work, breathing practice in Samiball is an indispensable tool for the understanding of the movements as it helps to focus the attention and perception of body consciousness.

Whether at the beginning or end of every session and whatever your level is, breathing practice is mandatory and indispensable. Breathing associated to Samiball method aims at awakening practitioners to a correct breathing and own conscience.

2.nd STAGE

EDUCATIONAL: the educational exercises are composed of conventional exercises and exercises inspired and adapted from yoga, capoeira, surfing and kitesurfing. All performed with the obligatory use of the Swiss ball in order to prepare all muscle groups for the next step. These exercises range from basic, moderate to advanced.

They are used both for rehabilitation and for prevention and training. However, the advanced ones involve more complex movements that only patients / students who are in good physical condition can do.

3.rd STAGE

TRANSITIONS: the third stage was called transitions as it involves movements that interconnect a primary position to another primary position for the purpose of communication between positions without losing body contact with the Swiss ball. These complex movements are made in three-dimensional form, performed on all planes and axes of the body. Transitions are usually found in the ramifications of the Samiball Method Art.

4.th STAGE

SEQUENCES: the fourth stage encompasses the sequences which are a set of postures made in a determined time in a single movement. It is performed in primary positions and aims at having the practitioner connecting one position to another.

BASIC SEQUENCE

Biomechanically analyzing the 11 postures of the Yoga Sun Salutation adapted to the Samiball® (Fig. 114), we can observe that the movements only occur in the sagittal and frontal planes, leaving the transverse plane aside as this sequence does not present any axial skeletal rotation.

Fig. 114

1.st Posture – Fig. 115: the practitioner is in an orthostatic position, erect spine with the hands joined to the front of the chest. The ball is touching the anterior and medial region of the leg and under pressure. The practitioner does a slight contraction of the abdomen and pelvic floor. Remember to do all the practice with this abdominal contraction.

Fig. 115

Muscular analysis of the 1st posture: initial position - Transervice of the abdomen (isometry), erector of the spine and paravertebrals . Lower limbs: Soleus, gastrocnemius and gluteus medius (by the support of the orthostatic position).

2.nd Posture – Fig. 116: shoulder abduction by touching the palms of the hands over the head, cervical extension and looking upwards.

Muscular analysis of the 2.nd posture: stretching of shoulder extensors and of the muscles that rotate down the scapula as well as flexors of the neck (anterior region).

Fig. 116

3.rd Posture – Fig. 117: exhale and flexion of the spine and hip (tilting arms and trunk forward), generating a tension to the entire posterior muscular chain. The practicioner touches the ball or the ground, looking downwards and having the forehead in contact with the ball.

Fig. 117

Muscular analysis of the 3.rd posture: stretching of the triceps surae, ischiastibias, erector spinae, multifidus and paravertebral.

4.th Posture – Fig. 118: inhale and extend the upper trunk having the spine aligned, extended knees and the transversus abdominis contracted.

Fig. 118

Muscular analysis of 4.th posture: stretching of ischiatibial and triceps surae and strengthening of spine extensors.

5.th Posture – Fig. 119: anterior region of the thigh in contact with the ball and hands on the ground. The practitioner remains in neutral extension of the spine supporting the trunk and performing an elbow flexion approaching the thorax to the ground.

Fig. 119

Muscular analysis of the 5.th posture: strengthening of the spine, shoulder girdle and flexor-extensors of the shoulder and elbow, passive stretching of the wrist flexors.

6.th Posture – Fig. 120: the practicioner flexes the shoulder and extends the elbow having the trunk pushing the ball back against the abdomen.

Muscular analysis of the 6.th posture: stretching of the muscles that flex the spine mainly in the abdominal rectus and strengthening of gluteus and spine extensors.

Fig. 120

7.th Posture – Fig. 121: inhale and raise the hip flexing the shoulder, touching the feet on the ground, looking towards the knees but remaining with the entire spine aligned (the ball may make it difficult to align the cervical). Heels to the ground while the torso and head remain lowered.

Fig. 121

Muscular analysis of the 7.th posture: stretching of the shoulders and hips extensors as well as triceps sural

8.th Posture – Fig. 122: inhale and perform a spine extension, leaving it aligned with knees extended, with the transversus abdominis contracted.

Fig. 122

Muscular analysis of the 8.th posture: stretching of the ischiatibial and triceps surae and strengthening of the spine extensors.

9.ᵗʰ Posture – Fig. 123: ehxale and flexes the spine and hip (tilting arms and trunk forward), generating a tension of the entire posterior muscular chain. Fingers touch the ball or the ground, looking downwards and the forehead in contact with the ball.

Fig. 123

Muscular analysis of the 9.ᵗʰ posture: stretching of shoulder and hips extensors as well as of the triceps surae.

10.ᵗʰ Posture – Fig. 124: perform an abduction of the shoulder by touching the palms of the hands over the head, extending the cervical and looking upwards.

Muscular analysis of the 10.ᵗʰ posture: stretching of the shoulder extensors, muscles that rotate down the scapula and the flexors of the neck (anterior region).

Fig. 124

5.ᵗʰ STAGE:

CHOREOGRAPHY: the fifth and final stage are the choreographies formed by a set of several sequences, derived from the primary positions and that takes transitions to connect one sequence to the other. It results in a continuous movement and in a harmonious connection. It may use songs to give the rhythm, resulting in an Art on the ball, expressed by capoeira or dancing.

CHAPTER 9

SAMIBALL® METHOD: REFLECTING ON THE DISCOVERY OF THE METHOD

Using researches based on empiricism, I understood that all my sources of inspiration are appreciated as Arts while they emerged as an attempt of human beings to express themselves through body techniques associated with mental activities. They can be used to free themselves of something or to unpack, each association having its particularity. All of these sources have had a huge influence on nature, specifically on the movements of animals. This may demonstrate how much we humans have strong connections with nature and animal life in general. We always have a lot to learn from them through coexistence, observation, contemplation and meditation. Great artists, masters and therapists have shown us this as they have had their great inspirations in these beings. Physical science itself and other branches such as biomechanics, through its early scholars (BORELLI, 1679; WEBER brothers, 1836 and MUYBRIDGE, 1887) was interested in studying the motility of animals and men due to their curiosity to analyze and understand living beings movements such as the flight of birds, the swimming of fish, jumping, squatting, man's sitting, human march, etc.

As yoga was mentioned in this book and its meaning represents union, integration; I was able to unite empirically and intuitively some body and mental techniques that already existed in human life. For this, I used only one resource – the Swiss ball. The other resources are already inherent to ourselves (the body is materialized energy and the mind is nonphysical energy).

I initially used the Swiss ball, which was first used for therapeutic and preventive purposes, as an object of play and exploration. Although I was a student of Physical Education and Physiotherapy at that time, 2004, I did not explore the existing literature on the subject because only a few books were translated and published in Brazil that time. However, as much as a book allows us to generate an infinity of knowledge, it can also be limited by the content of it. This may be a factor to determine imagination, experimentation and practical creation as it offers the exercises to be studied and practiced several times.

I hereby reinforce this idea by citing one of the theories of motor development (THELEN, 1991 apud GONÇALVES, 1995). The Theory of Dynamic Systems. This theory recognizes the maturation stage of the Central Nervous System (CNS) is an important factor for the emergence of motor skills. However, as it is considered a holistic model, this theory is based on three components: the individual, the environment and the functional task. In this case here, the individual was me; the environment was formed by my past experiences and the experiences with the ball and the functional task was the interaction with the ball. The result of this combination is the movement. Such components acting together contribute to the development of a certain skill, and the three components originate a certain motor behavior. Each of these factors may exert limitations on the onset and performance of motor skills.

By constantly practicing the exercises with the ball and associating the breathing techniques and relaxation techniques from yoga, I was able to experience some meditative states. In Tibetan meditation means "becomes familiar" (RINPOCHE et all, 2008). From this, innumerable possibilities of movement were developed in the course of my studies. Therefore, I became a Swiss ball enthusiast instigated by the curiosity of practical contact. Through the interaction with the ball I created new expressions, knowledge, thus expanding the state of the art regarding to the Swiss ball as a subject. I realized that certain exercises could be damaging, and harmful what is similar to sports and body arts where certain postures and movements can really be harmful to the body.

I offer new models and new lines of applicability to this object and no longer just as exercises for therapeutic, preventive and preparatory uses. I also see it as a resource for corporal expression and consciousness expansion, creating personal development connected to the playful and tied to Arts. Therefore, I hope that this book serves as a gateway for you reader, who seeks to go deeper and look for other sources cited in the book, on subjects related to self-knowledge, therapy by movement and body expressions linked to the sources of inspiration of the method.

CHAPTER 10

EXERCISES ON THE BALL: INTRODUCTION

The exercises illustrated below work on several joint segments at the same time, as a result of increased muscle group demands. According to Platonov, (1995) general action exercises work great part of the muscular mass of the body, involving large muscle groups, providing an adequate stimulus to the cardiovascular system and to metabolism.

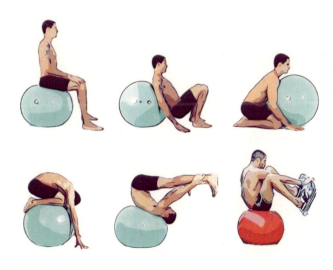

These exercises can be performed repetitively with low, moderate or high intensity or with a permanence time varied depending on the way they are performed and the goals that are set, allowing for increased flexibility, balance, muscle strength, as well as the increased use of energy by muscles.

Kisner, (2005) argues that this increased energy use may be a direct result of high levels of oxidative enzymes in muscles, as well as increased mitochondrial density and size and capillary supply in muscle fibers, resulting in fatigue resistance, enabling the individual to work for extended periods of time.

These exercises work the axial skeleton combined with the appendicular skeleton in a synchronous, symmetrical and / or asymmetric way, promoting a motor coordination, this will contribute to the accomplishment of uniform, precise and controlled movements. These movements involve a muscular co-contraction, that is, reciprocal activation of the agonists and antagonists, in addition working with the anticipatory activity.

According to Borges *et al* (2005), this anticipated activity is the activation of the accessory muscles to generate the dynamic stability during the agonists' contraction of the movement, being an indispensable biomechanics mechanism in which the agonist muscles work more efficiently during the movement. In addition, it involves the proper synchronization of synergic muscle activity and establishes stability of the proximal segment along body balance, by keeping the center of gravity on the base of unstable support (ball).

Each exercise contains a kinesiological analysis, in order to facilitate the understanding of joint movements with muscle activation but not all the muscles of the human body are mentioned only the necessary ones for the accomplishment of the movements.

NOTE: Some exercises shown below have the same name as some yoga and capoeira postures and kite and surf moves for resembling the same. These exercises are of utmost importance to all people working with the body, whether through rehabilitation, prevention, physical exercise, sports training or art. It seems that it is good to make it clear that there are movements that are of high complexity, and that what I meant was to make it easy understanding of the body on the ball. However, some movements are **not indicated** for people who are not able to perform because they demand a lot from body structures and abilities such as the heart, intracranial pressure, joints, balance and resistance, among many others.

Nevertheless, it is essential and mandatory that the professional has a Samiball method training course and also a good experience in teaching exercises to feel their effects and thus be able and conscious to choose, teach or transmit the exercises to their patients, students, athletes or artists. They should always monitor their feedback so that they are not harmful, because the intention of this wide range of illustrated movements is to show how much we can exercise in a different way using the Swiss ball.

SEATED EDUCATIONAL EXERCISES

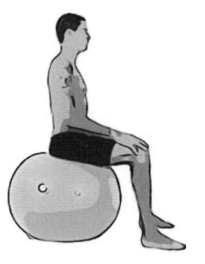

The exercises illustrated below are made in the primary sitting position in which the starting position will always have the feet and the ball as a base of support, and counted body in the ball will be the ischia. Some of these exercises have been taken from literature and while the other exercises are part of the Samiball methodology and were created from other inspiring sources. It is always good to observe and analyze these exercises in order to be applied correctly, because depending on the patient, student and practitioner there may be some contraindication. Most of these exercises present a kinesiological analysis containing information such as: the achievement of movement, positions and joint movements, activated muscles and goals. All to help a better understanding for the reader.

BASIC POINTS

Some observations of the sitting position

Ideal Joint Positions for the SAMIBALL® Method

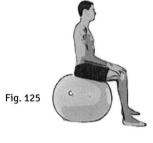

Fig. 125 – 90° of hip flexion.

- 90° to 110° of knee flexion.

- Heel with a certain distance from the ball to get more basis support.

Fig. 125

Points with some changes in joint angulation

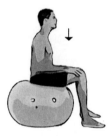

Fig. 126 – Deflatted ball.

- Lower center of gravity.

- Greater contact area from the ball with the ground.

- It requires less balance.

- Greater hip flexion.

Fig. 126

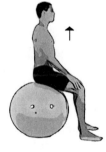

Fig. 127 – Over inflated ball.

- Hip angle less than 90°.

- Less contact from the ball with the ground.

- It requires greater balance.

- It generates pelvic anteversion and lower hip flexion.

Fig. 127

BALANCE EXERCISES (CONVENTIONAL ONES)

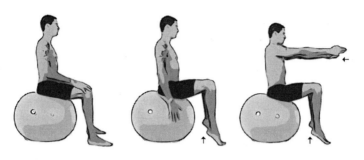

Fig. 128   Fig. 130

Fig. 129

Initial position (sitting with bipodal support)

Fig. 131   Fig. 133

Fig. 132

Sitting on the ball and with contact of metatarsals tip on the ground and with hands on the ball (Fig. 129).

Sitting on the ball and with contact of metatarsals tip on the ground without hands on the ball (Fig. 130).

Initial position with one-leg support and one knee extended (Fig. 131).

Sitting on the ball with unipodal support and contact of metatarsals on the ground with their hands on the ball (Fig. 132).

Sitting on the ball and with unipodal support and contact of the metatarsals on the ground, without hands on the ball (Fig. 133).

Variation

Initial position with unipodal support and with one knee flexed and the feet on the other thigh, with the hands in the ball (Fig. 134).

Sitting unipodal support and with one knee flexed and feet on the other thigh, with hands on the ball, perform an exhalation and flexes the spine (Fig. 135).

Fig. 134   Fig. 135

LEVEL AND GOALS:

- Basic and moderate movement (variation).

- Movement in the sagittal plane;

- Work the postural reactions (balance, rectification and straightening);

- Promote activation of the trunk muscles (abdominals and extensors) mainly in the postures without the support of the hands in the ball;

- Promote isometric activation and strengthening of the elevated leg hip flexors;

- Promote isometric activation and strengthening of the plantar flexors in the postures with support at the fingertips;

- Promote elongation of the spinal extensors during flexion of the spine.

BOUNCER JUMPER ON THE BALL (CONVENTIONAL MOVES)

Fig. 136   Fig. 137

MOVEMENTS AND ARTICULAR POSITIONS

- Cervical, thoracic and lumbar spine: Traction and compression of the vertebrae.

- Shoulder: neutral position.

- Elbow: slight flexion in transition for extension.

- Hip: mild flexion in transition to extension.

- Knee: mild flexion in transition to extension.

- Ankle: mild Plantar and dorsal flexion.

MOVEMENT EXECUTION: the practitioner makes a movement up and down, with a slight extension and flexion of the hip and knee, without losing the contact of the feet in the ground.

ACTIVATED MUSCLES: TRUNK: Paravertebrais, rectus abdominis, obliques, spine erectors. LOWER LIMBS: Iliopsoas, pectineus, rectus femoris, semimembranosus, semitendinosus, femoral biceps, quadriceps, calf and anterior tibialis.

LEVEL AND GOALS:

- Movement Basic level;

- Perform the movement in the sagittal plane;

- Work on postural reactions;

- Promote activation of the abdominal, paravertebral, flexor and extensor muscles of the hip, knee and ankle muscles;

- Mobilize hip and knee in flexion and extension;

- Traction the spine by moving up and down;

- Work Balance and Fitness.

PELVIC ANTEVERSION AND RETROVERSION
(conventional ones)

Movement performed with abduction and horizontal adduction of the UPPER LIMBS.

Fig. 138

Variation with the UPPER LIMBS in shoulder flexion with the arms at the front of the body.

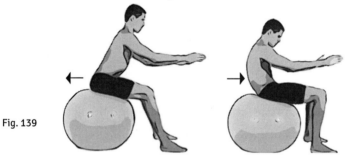

Fig. 139

Variation of pelvic movement on the diagonal.

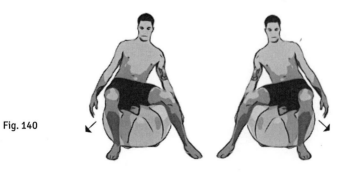

Fig. 140

MOVEMENTS AND ARTICULAR POSITIONS

- Cervical, thoracic: neutral column; Lumbar: from extension in transition to flexion.
- Hip: mild flexion in transition to extension (fig. 140).
- Knee: mild flexion in transition to extension.
- Ankle: slight plantar flexion in transition to Dorsiflexion.

MOVEMENT EXECUTION: practitioner performs a pelvic anteversion movement with the upper limbs in horizontal adduction and then does a pelvic retroversion with the upper limbs in horizontal abduction, the movement is performed by pushing the ball back and forth.

ACTIVATED MUSCLES: TRUNK/pelvic Waist: On retroversion: Paravertebrais, erector spine, lumbar square. In anteversion: rectus abdominis, obliques, iliopsoas, rectus femoris proximal portion, gluteus maximus, medium. UPPER LIMBS: In horizontal adduction: pectoralis major, coracobrachial, biceps, brachial, anterior deltoid and major round. In horizontal abduction: posterior deltoid, rhomboids, trapezoid medium and inferior fibers. LOWER LIMBS: Hamstrus, rectus femoris, Sartorius, calf.

LEVEL AND GOALS:

- Basic movements;
- Movement performed in the sagittal plane;
- Work on postural reactions;
- Performs activation of the abdominal and pelvic muscles;
- Strengthens the abdominal muscles. (Mainly the rectus abdominis lower portion);

- Mobilizes the lumbar spine, hip, knee and flexion and extension, and the pelvic girdle in retroversion and anteversion;
- Mobilizes the shoulder in abduction and horizontal adduction;
- Works balance and motor coordination;

LATERAL PELVIC BENDING

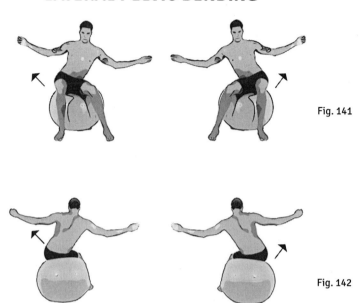

Fig. 141

Fig. 142

MOVEMENTS AND ARTICULAR POSITIONS

- Lumbar Spine: right pelvic tilt along with lateral flexion of the lower torso to right in transition to Left pelvic tilt with flexion lat. left.

- Shoulder: abduction.

- Elbow: slight flexion.

- Hip: mild abduction in transition for bilateral adduction alternately.

- Knee: mild flexion accompanied by rot. .nt. in transition to rot. bilateral ext. with flexion.

MOVEMENT EXECUTION: the practitioner performs a lateral pelvic tilt movement to the right and left side with the abduction UPPER LIMBS, pushing the ball to one side and the other.

ACTIVATED MUSCLES: TRUNK: rectus abdominis unilateral inclination, internal and external oblique, unilateral lumbar spine to inclination, paravertebral and erector spine; UPPER LIMBS: Cuff rotators, deltoid lateral and posterior fibers, rhomboids and trapezius middle and lower fibers with more emphasis on the slope side. LOWER LIMBS: short, long, magnus and gluteus maximus adductor, minimum, maximum and tensor from fascia to can.

LEVEL AND GOALS:

- Basic movement;
- Perform balance movement in the frontal plane;
- Mobilize cabbage. lumbar flexion in lateral flexion / pelvic tilt;
- Mobilize the lateral muscles of the lower torso;
- Mobilizes hips in adduction and abduction;
- Activation and strengthening of lateral trunk muscles;
- Promote typical gait movements by lifting the pelvis;
- Promote Equilibrium and Coordination.

PELVIC CIRCUNDUCTION

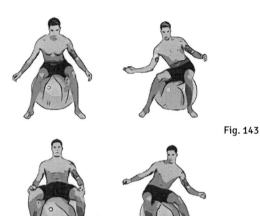

Fig. 143

MOVEMENTS AND ARTICULAR POSITIONS

- Lumbar Spine: anteversion in transition to pelvic tilt left. then does a retroversion in transition to pelvic tilt to dir. in a circular motion.

- Shoulder: bilateral abduction.

- Elbow: slight bilateral flexion.

- Handle: neutral or slightly bent position.

- Hip: movements of flexion, abduction, adduction and mild bilateral extension.

- Knee: combined movements slight flexion in transition to extension with rot. Internal right and outer rot. left in transition to rot. external right and internal rot. left.

- Ankle: combined movements of dorsal flexion, plantar, inversion and eversion.

MOVEMENT EXECUTION: the practitioner performs a circular movement of the pelvic waist performing a slight circular movement of the ball on the ground.

ACTIVATED MUSCLES: TRUNK: straight abdomen, oblique internal and external, lumbar square, paravertebral, spinal erector. LOWER LIMBS: adductor short, long, magnus and gluteus medius, minimum and maximum, iliopsoas, rectus femoris, soleus, gastrocnemius, anterior tibial, fibular.

LEVEL AND GOALS:

- Movement - Basic level;
- Perform balance movement in the frontal plane and sagittal or obliquely;
- Mobilize the lumbar spine and flexion / extension and Lateral Flexion. Left and Right;
- Mobilize the pelvis in anteversion-retroversion / right lateral inclination. and left;
- Activate all the muscles of the trunk of the anterior, posterior and lateral region;
- Promote balance and coordination.

SIDE SHIFT OF THE GLUTEES WITH TRUNK ROTATION
BODYSPHERES by Mari Naumovski

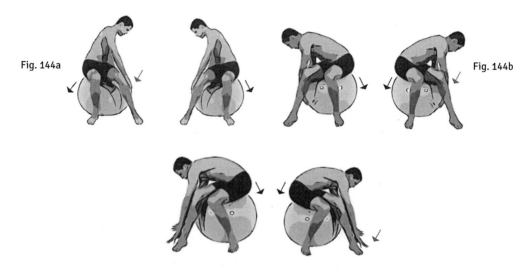

Fig. 144a   Fig. 144b

Fig. 144c

MOVEMENTS AND ARTICULAR POSITIONS

- Thoracic and lumbar spine: combined rotation movement accompanied by flexion progressing the amplitude.

- Shoulders: bilateral flexion.

- Pelvic girdle: lateral inclination at right in transition to left lateral tilt.

- Hip: combined movement of flexion, abduction and right and left adduction alternately.

- Knee: flexion accompanied by internal rotation in transition to flexion and alternating external rotation.

- Ankle: combined movements of dorsal flexion, plantar, inversion and eversion.

MOVEMENT EXECUTION: the practitioner performs a movement of pelvis displacement out of the ball performing a flexion with rotation of the spine and accompanied by a flexion and extension of the hip and knee.

ACTIVATED MUSCLES: TRUNK: straight abdomen, oblique internal and external, lumbar square, paravertebral, spinal erector. UPPER LIMBS: trapezius medium and inferior fibers, pectoralis major, anterior deltoid, large dorsal, triceps, all bilateral anechoic. LOWER LIMBS: adductor short, long, magnus and gluteus medius, minimum and maximum, iliopsoas, rectus femoris, soleus, gastrocnemius, anterior tibial, fibular.

GOALS

- Movement - Basic to Moderate Level;
- Movement performed in the frontal plane and transverse or oblique plane;
- Mobilize the thoracic and lumbar spine in flexion and rotation and the pelvic girdle in pelvic tilt to the right and left sides;
- Activates the rotator muscles and trunk flexors;
- Promote dislocation movements of the shoulder girdle;
- Promote balance and coordination;
- Work on muscular and cardiopulmonary resistance when repeated several times.

JUMPING SIDEWAYS

Fig. 145

MOVEMENTS AND ARTICULAR POSITIONS

- Lumbar Spine: right lateral flexion in transition to left lateral tilt.

- Shoulder: from the adduction position to a slight extension of the limb that is in the hand rest on ball.

- Wrist and fingers: transitional flexion for extension of the hand that rests on the ball.

- Pelvic girth: light Pelvic tilt from right to transition to mild left pelvic tilt.

- Hip: lightly bending in transition to light extension to raise feet off the ground.

- Knee: mild flexion in transition to extension.

- Ankle: combined eversion movements for inversion.

MOVEMENT EXECUTION: sitting on the ball, it carries weight transfer laterally removing the feet from the ground, sliding the gluteus on the ball from side to side.

ACTIVATED MUSCLES: TRUNK: oblique internal and external, lumbar square, rectus abdominis, spine erectors. UPPER LIMBS.: rhomboids, trapezius medium and inferior fibers, deltoid lateral fibers, large round, large dorsal. LOWER LIMBS: iliopssoas, rectus femoris, adductors, abductors, soleus, gastrognemius, tibialis anterior.

GOALS

- Movement with a moderate level of execution;
- Perform balance movement in the frontal plane;
- Mobilize the lumbar spine lateral flexion and pelvic tilt of right for left;
- Promote weight transfer sideways;
- Promote more balance and coordination by withdrawing feet on the ground;
- Assist in automatic balancing reactions;
- Work on muscular and cardiopulmonary resistance when repeated in a given time.

GLUTEUS LATERAL GLIDING WITH HAND ON THE FLOOR

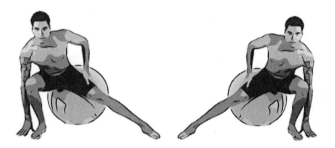

Fig. 146

GLUTEUS LATERAL GLIDING WITH HAND ON THE FLOOR

- Cervical Column: Neutral; Thoracic and Lumbar: flexion.
- Shoulder: light flexion (hand on the ground) in transition to extension (thigh hand) alternating bilaterally.
- Elbow: transition flexion for bilateral alternating extension.
- Wrist and fingers: bilateral extension.
- Hip: flexion (flexion knee) in transition for abduction (extended knee) alternating.
- Knee: flexion in transition for extension of alternating form.
- Ankle: combined movements of plantar flexion for eversion.

MOVEMENT EXECUTION: sitting on the ball, slide the ball to the side, abducting the hip and extending the knee, then place the palm of the hand on the ground near the side of the foot.

ACTIVATED MUSCLES: TRUNK: abdomen straight, bilateral oblique lateral lumbar ipislateral hand supporting on the ground. UPPER LIMBS: Deltoid, coracobrachial, pectoralis major, biceps long portion, triceps, anecdotal, wrist extensors. LOWER LIMBS: iliopsoas, rectus femoris, ischium proximal portion.

LEVEL AND GOALS:

- Movement with a basic level in execution;
- Perform balance movement in the frontal plane;
- Mobilize the lumbar spine in lumbar flexion;
- Mobilize the hips joint in abduction and flexion and knees in extension and flexion;
- Promote stretching of knee thigh adductors extended;
- Promote elongation of the ankle eversors;
- Work balance and coordination.

GLUTEUS LATERAL GLIDING WITH TRUNK ROTATION

Fig. 147

Fig. 148

MOVEMENT AND JOINT POSITIONS

- Cervical, thoracic and lumbar spine: combined bending movements, lateral flexion accompanied by rotation for both sides.

- Shoulder: horizontal abduction.

- Elbow: flexion in transition for extension when supported by hand on the ground.

- Wrist and fingers: bending in transition to extend the hand that supports the ground.

- Hip: combined flexion and abduction movements.

- Knee: bending movements in transition to stretch alternately.

- Ankle: dorsal flexion in transition for alternating eversion.

MOVEMENT EXECUTION: sitting on the ball, slide the ball to the side, extending the knee and abducting the hip of the lower limb, then place the palm of the right hand on the ground and make a rotation of the column to the left pointing the left hand to top.

ACTIVATED MUSCLES: TRUNK: cervical rotators, internal and external oblique, bilateral lumbar square, rectus abdominis and erector spine unilateral to inclination, rotators. UPPER LIMBS: Trapezium, rhomboids, deltoid, bilateral major round, pectoralis major, rotator cuff, coracobrachial, biceps brachii, brachial (of the arm supported on the ground) LOWER LIMBS: Max, medial and minimum gluteus, fascia a cantay tensor, inverters

LEVEL AND GOALS:

- Movement with a moderate level of execution;
- Perform balance movement in the frontal plane;
- Perform motion in the oblique plane;
- Mobilize the lumbar spine in lateral flexion and flexion and rotation more emphasis on the sides of the trunk;
- Mobilize the hip joint in abduction and flexion;
- Promote spinal rotation movements;
- Promote stretching of thigh adductors;
- Promote elongation of spinal rotators (variation).

GINGAR WITH A FOOT POSTERIORIZATION

Fig. 149

Variation with the hand on the ball and the other in front of the face

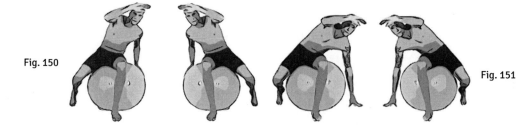

Fig. 150

Fig. 151

MOVEMENTS AND ARTICULAR POSITIONS

- Cervical, thoracic and lumbar spine: slight lateral flexion progressing for flexion, lateral flexion and rotation according to the evolution of the postures.

- Shoulder: initially placed in two members in horizontal abduction (Fig. 149), progressing from flexion (hand to front of head) to extension (hand supported on the ball (Fig. 150 and 151) according to the evolution of the postures.

- Elbow: flexion combined with slight extension (Fig. 151)

- Wrist and fingers: neutral position or slight flexion in transition for extension when resting on the ball or on the ground.

- Hip: flexion (limb with foot in front of ball) in transition to slight extension with abduction (limb with foot on side of ball).
- Knee: flexion in transition for slight extension.
- Ankle: dorsal flexion (foot that is in front of the ball) in transition to plantar flexion (of the foot that is laterally in the ball).

MOVEMENT EXECUTION: the practitioner performs the lateral movement of the lower trunk as a hip on the ball, changing the lower limbs. The foot that was in front of the ball goes to the side and back and what was behind comes forward of the bal. The trunk makes a slight flexion accompanied by lateral flexion, the upper limbs in a horizontal abduction of the shoulder and slight elbow flexion without the hand's back to the ball. This can evolve according to Fig. 150 and 151. (Hand rest on ball or ground).

ACTIVATED MUSCLES: (because it involves multiple joints, several muscles are works by co-contraction citing only a few). TRUNK: internal and external oblique's, lumbar square, spine erectors on the side of the concavity. UPPER LIMBS: Column: Deltoid, pectoralis major, coracobrachial, biceps brachia and brachialis, brachioradialis (member in front of head); posterior and medial deltoid, rhomboids, trapezius medial fibers, minor round (limb that is supported on the ball or ground). LOWER LIMBS: iliopsoas, rectus femoris, tensor from fascia to can, gluteus maximus, quadriceps (limb that is in front of the ball); gluteus maximus, gluteus medius posterior fibers, ischiostibial (limb on the side of the ball).

LEVEL AND GOALS:

- Movement - Moderate level;
- Perform balance movement performed in the frontal plane and obliquely;
- Practice reactive steps from side to side;
- Mobilize the lumbar spine in lateral flexion and pelvis in pelvic tilt;
- Promote weight transfer sideways;
- Promote more balance and coordination by removing feet off the ground;
- Promote hip extension;
- Includes reciprocal movements of upper limbs and lower limbs required for walking;
- Assist in automatic balancing reactions;
- Perform mobilization of the shoulder girdle;
- Dissociate the shoulder girdle;
- Increase the amplitude of the column in flexion and rotation;
- Increase hip amplitude in flexion and extension;
- Work on muscular and cardiopulmonary resistance when repeated in a given time.

LATERO-LATERAL GINGAR

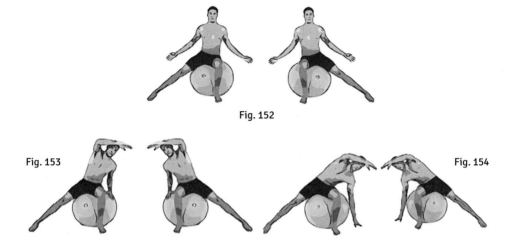

Fig. 152

Fig. 153

Fig. 154

Variation with the Hand on the ball and in front of the face

MOVEMENTS AND ARTICULAR POSITIONS

- Cervical, thoracic and lumbar spine: slight lateral flexion progressing in transition to lateral flexion with greater amplitude according to the evolution of the postures.

- Shoulder: initially abducted horizontally, progressing flexion of the limb with the forearm in front of the head and extension of the limb that is supported on the ball or on the ground, according to the progressions of the postures.

- Elbow: slight extension in transition for mild bilateral flexion.

- Wrist and fingers: flexion in transition for extension when supported by hand on ball or ground.

- Hip: flexion (limb with foot in front of ball) for extension with abduction (limb with foot on side of ball).

- Knee: flexion in transition for slight extension.

- Ankle: dorsal flexion of the foot that is in front of the ball in transition for plantar flexion of the foot that is laterally in the ball.

MOVEMENT EXECUTION: the practitioner performs the lateral movement of the hip by exchanging the lower limbs, in which the flexed limb extends and abducts in the same line of the opposite foot in a laterolateral movement. The trunk makes a lateral flexion for the extended limb and upper limbs in a slight extension of the shoulder and slight elbow flexion without touching the hand on the ball.

ACTIVATED MUSCLES: TRUNK: oblique internal and external, lumbar square, spine erectors side of concavity of spine. UPPER LIMBS: deltoid, pectoralis major, coracobrachial, biceps brachii and brachialis, brachioradialis (member that is in front of the head); posterior and medial deltoid, rhomboids, trapezius medial fibers, smaller round and wrist and finger extensors. (a member that is supported on the ball or ground); LOWER LIMBS: iliopsoas, rectus femoris, tensor from fascia to can, gluteus maximus, quadriceps (limb that is in front of the ball); gluteus maximus, gluteus medius and minis, ischiostibial, quadriceps (limb that is on the side of the ball.

LEVEL AND GOALS:

- Perform balance movement in the frontal and transverse plane.
- Weight transfer laterally;
- Practice reactive steps from side to side;
- Mobilize the lumbar spine in lateral flexion and pelvic tilt.
- Promote weight transfer sideways;
- Promote more balance and coordination by withdrawing feet on the ground;
- Promote hip abduction and flexion of the opposite;

- Includes reciprocal movements of upper and lower limbs necessary to march;
- Assist in automatic balancing reactions;
- Perform mobilization of the shoulder girdle;
- Dissociate the shoulder girdle;
- Increase the amplitude of the column in flexion and rotation;
- Increase hip amplitude in abduction and adduction;
- Promote more coordination due to the simultaneous work of the upper limbs with the lower limbs;
- Promote physical fitness.

ROTACIONAL

Fig. 155

MOVEMENTS AND ARTICULAR POSITIONS

- Cervical, thoracic and lumbar spine: neutral position for flexion with rotation.

- Shoulder: horizontal abduction in transition for Left adduction and Right extension.

- Elbow: extension of the left and extension in transition for flexion of the right hand supported on the ball.

- Fist and fingers: neutral in transition for extension of the hand supported on the ball.

- Hip: transition flexion for right adduction and left abduction with flexion.

- Knee: increases flexion with external rotation of left and extension of right.

MOVEMENT EXECUTION: with the upper limbs in horizontal abduction the practitioner initiates the movement with a rotation of the trunk accompanied by slight flexion, trying to touch the left hand on the right foot, the other shoulder in extension with his hand on the ball.

ACTIVATED MUSCLES: TRUNK: rectum abdominal, obliquus internal and external, paravertebral, spinal erector of the side of the rotation. UPPER LIMBS: pectoralis major, coracobrachial, triceps, anechoic of the Left limb. deltoid posterior, rhomboids, trapezius fibers, anterior serratil of the limb supported on the ball. LOWER LIMBS: gluteus medius, fascia a tensor, hamstrings, rectus femoris origin of the right limb, long adductor, short, magno, pectus hamstrings of the left limb.

LEVEL AND GOALS:

- Perform balance movement in the frontal, sagittal and transverse plane;
- Promote slight dissociation of waists;
- Mobilize the lumbar spine in flexion and rotation;
- Promote stretching of the posterior leg muscles extended;
- Mobilize the scapula in adduction and bilateral abduction;
- Assist in automatic equilibrium reaction.

BALANCE WITH THE ISCHIOS

Fig. 156

MOVEMENTS AND ARTICULAR POSITIONS

- Cervical, thoracic and lumbar spine: slight flexion.
- Shoulder: extension.
- Elbow: flexion.
- Fist and fingers: extension.
- Hip: bending movement allowing feet to be withdrawn from the ground.
- Knee: flexion.
- Ankle: neutral position.

MOVEMENT EXECUTION: sitting on the ball, the person during inspiration draws one foot off the ground and then withdraws the other foot, keeping the ischia in the ball, thus maintaining balance

ACTIVATED MUSCLES: TRUNK: rectus abdominis lower portion, internal and external obliquus, and paravertebrae. UPPER LIMBS: Romboids, trapezium-medial fibers, rotator cuff, deltoid posterior fibers, triceps long portion. LOWER LIMBS: rectus femoris, iliopsoas, tensor of fascia a lata, adductors.

LEVEL AND GOALS:

- Perform movement in the sagittal plane;
- Work the postural reactions;
- Promote stretching of the flexors of the shoulder in a closed chain;
- Promote isometric strengthening of the lower abdominal and hip flexor muscles in the open chain;
- Activate the entire trunk musculature and limbs;
- Promote balance.

LIGHT FLEXION AND EXTENSION OF THE HIP WITH A FLEXED KNEE

Fig. 157

MOVEMENTS AND ARTICULAR POSITIONS

- Column: light flexion.
- Shoulder: bilateral extension.
- Elbow: extension.
- Fist and fingers: extension.
- Hip: extension in transition for flexion.
- Knee: flexion.
- Ankle: plantar flexion.

MOVEMENT EXECUTION: sitting in the ball with the shoulders in hyperextension, with the hands in the ground, the practitioner performs a slight flexion and extension of 45 degrees of the hip.

ACTIVATED MUSCLES: TRUNK: rectus abdominis lower portion, bilateral oblique internal and external. UPPER LIMBS: Deltoid posterior fibers (rotator cuff) major and minor round, rhomboids, trapezius, triceps, ankle, wrist extensors and fingers (isometry). LOWER LIMBS: femoral rectus, iliopsoas, fascia to can tensor, max., (isotonia), soleus, bilateral gastrocnemius (isometric), short adductor, long magnus, pectin (isometry).

LEVEL AND GOALS:

- Perform movement in the frontal plane;
- Work the postural reactions;
- Promotes isometric strengthening give cervical flexors;
- Promote elongation of the shoulder flexors and elbow flexors;
- Promote balance;
- Isometric strengthening of closed-chain upper limbs;
- Strengthening of the abdominal and hip flexors in the open chain.

LIGHT (ALTERNATED) FLEXION AND EXTENSION OF THE HIP WITH A FLEXED KNEE

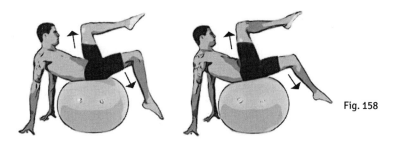

Fig. 158

MOVEMENTS AND ARTICULAR POSITIONS

- Column: light bending.
- Shoulder: bilateral extension.
- Elbow: extension.
- Fist and fingers: extension.
- Hip: extension in transition for flexion with alternating movement of the limbs.
- Knee: flexion.
- Ankle: plantar flexion.

MOVEMENT EXECUTION: sitting on the ball with the shoulders in hyperextension, with hands on the ground, the practitioner performs a 90° flexion and extension approximately 180° of the hip with the knee flexed.

ACTIVATED MUSCLES: TRUNK: cervical region: platysma, bilateral complex hyoid (isometric), rectus abdominis inferior portion, and internal and external obliquus. UPPER LIMBS: deltoid posterior fibers, (major and minor round rotator cuff, rhomboids, trapezius, triceps, anecdotal, wrist extensors and fingers. LOWER LIMBS (Isotopic), adductor (isometric), soleus, bilateral gastrocnemius (isometric), ischemia, proximal (isotonic).

LEVEL AND GOALS:

- Perform movement in the frontal plane;
- Work the postural reactions;
- Promotes motor coordination of the lower limbs by alternate movement;
- Promote isometric strengthening give cervical flexors;
- Promote elongation of the shoulder flexors and elbow flexors;
- Isometric strengthening of closed-chain upper limb;
- Promote strengthening of the lower abdominal muscles, rectus femoris iliopsoas open chain;
- Promote balance.

(ALTERNATED) FLEXION AND EXTENSION OF THE HIP WITH AN EXTENDED KNEE

Fig. 159

MOVEMENTS AND ARTICULAR POSITIONS

- Cervical spine: Thoracic and Lumbar flexion: slight flexion.
- Shoulder: bilateral extension.
- Elbow: extension.
- Fist and fingers: extension.
- Hip: extension in transition for flexion with alternating limbs.
- Knee: extension.
- Ankle: plantar flexion.

MOVEMENT EXECUTION: sitting on the ball with the shoulders in hyperextension, hands on the ground, the practitioner performs a 90° flexion and 180° extension of the hip alternately from the limbs.

ACTIVATED MUSCLES: TRUNK: rectus abdominis lower portion, oblique internal and external. UPPER LIMBS: deltoid posterior fibers (rotator cuff) major and minor round, rhomboids, trapezius, triceps, anecdotal, wrist extensors and fingers (isometric) LOWER LIMBS: femoral rectus, iliopsoas, fascia to tensor, maximus, medius and minimus gluteus; adductors and plantar flexors (isometric).

LEVEL AND GOALS:

- Perform movement in the frontal plane;
- Promote greater resistance arm by lower limbs for having knee extension;
- Work the postural reactions. (balance, straightening and rectification);
- Promotes isometric strengthening give cervical flexors;
- Promote elongation of the shoulder flexors and elbow flexors;
- Promote an isometric contraction of the closed-arm shoulder extensors;
- Promote an isometric contraction of the knee extensors;
- Promote strengthening of the flexors of the open chain hip;
- Promote strengthening of the lower abdominal muscles;
- Promote Balance.

FLEXION AND EXTENSION OF THE HIP WITH AN EXTENDED KNEE

Fig. 160

MOVEMENTS AND JOINT POSITIONS

- Cervical column: flexion; thoracic and lumbar: light flexion extension for flexion.
- Shoulder: bilateral extension.
- Elbow: extension.
- Fist and fingers: extension.
- Hip: extension in transition for flexion.
- Knee: extension.
- Ankle: plantar flexion.

MOVEMENT EXECUTION: sitting on the ball with the shoulders in hyperextension, with hands on the ground, the practitioner performs a 90° flexion and extension of approximately 180° of the hip.

ACTIVATED MUSCLES: TRUNK: rectus abdominis lower portion, oblique internal and external. UPPER LIMBS: deltoid posterior fibers (rotator cuff) major and minor round, rhomboids, trapezius, triceps, anecdotal, wrist extensors and fingers (isometric) LOWER

LIMBS: femoral rectus, iliopsoas, fascia to tensor, gluteus maximus, medius and minimus; adductors and plantar flexors (isometric).

LEVEL AND GOALS:

- Perform movement in the frontal plane;
- Promote greater resistance arm by the lower limbs for having knees in extension;
- Work the postural reactions;
- Promote elongation of the shoulder flexors;
- Promote isometric strengthening of closed-arm shoulder extensors;
- Promote lower abdominal muscles strengthening;
- Promote strengthening of the flexor muscles of the hip in an open chain;
- Promote balance.

INFERIOR TRUNK ROTATION WITH FLEXED KNEES

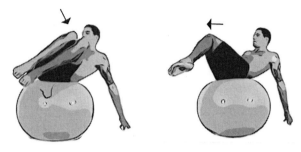

Fig. 161

MOVEMENTS AND ARTICULAR POSITIONS

- Cervical and thoracic spine: slight flexion; Lumbar Spine: rotation from right in transition to left (lower torso).
- Shoulder: extension.
- Elbow: extension.
- Fist and fingers: extension.
- Hip: adduction.
- Knee: flexion.
- Ankle: plantar flexion.

MOVEMENT EXECUTION: sitting on the ball with the shoulders in hyperextension, with the hands on the ground, the practitioner realizes a rotation of the inferior trunk with the hip in adduction.

ACTIVATED MUSCLES: TRUNK: straight abdomen lower portion, internal and external obliquus and paravertebrais. UPPER LIMBS: deltoid posterior fibers, (major and minor round rotator cuff, rhomboids, trapezius, triceps, anecdotal, wrist extensors and fingers. LOWER LIMBS: rectus femoris, iliopsoas and hamstrings (bilateral isometric), fascia to tensor, maxillary, medullary and minimum glutes of abduction limb and adductor limb adductors.

LEVEL AND GOALS:

- Promote lateral-lateral weight transfer;
- Perform movement in the oblique plane;
- Work on postural reactions;
- Promote a smaller lever arm by the lower limbs for having knees in flexion;
- Promote isometric strengthening of closed shoulder and elbow extensors;
- Promote elongation of the flexors of the shoulder and the elbow;
- Promote strengthening of the lower abdominal muscles, especially rotators and closed-loop flexors;
- Promote balance.

INFERIOR TRUNK ROTATION WITH EXTENDED KNEES

Fig. 162

MOVEMENTS AND JOINT POSITIONS

- Cervical and thoracic spine: slight flexion; Lumbar Column: rotation from right in transition to rotation to left (lower torso).
- Shoulder: extension.
- Elbow: extension.
- Fist and fingers: extension.
- Hip: adduction.
- Knee: extension.
- Ankle: plantar flexion.

MOVEMENT EXECUTION: sitting on the ball with the shoulders in hyperextension, with the hands on the ground, the practitioner realizes a rotation of the lower trunk.

ACTIVATED MUSCLES: TRUNK: rectus abdominis lower portion, internal and external obliquus, and paravertebrae. UPPER LIMBS: deltoid posterior fibers (rotator cuff) major and minor, rhomboids, trapezius, triceps, anecdotal, wrist and finger extensors (isometric) LOWER LIMBS: femoral rectus, iliopsoas and quadriceps (bilateral isometric), fascia a can, gluteus medius and minimum of the abduction limb and adductor limb adductors.

LEVEL AND GOALS:

- Perform movement in the transverse plane;
- Work the postural reactions;
- Promote greater resistance arm by the lower limbs for having knees in extension;
- Promote elongation of the shoulder flexors;
- Promote lower abdominal muscles strengthening;
- Promote balance;
- Promote strengthening of the flexor (isometric), abductors and adductors (isotonic) muscles of the open-chain hip;
- Promote balance.

FEET TO HAND SUPPORT TRANSFERENCE

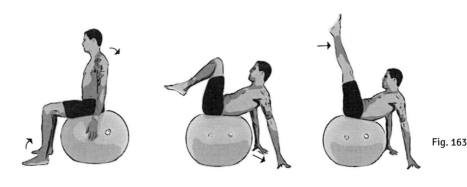

Fig. 163

MOVEMENTS AND ARTICULAR POSITIONS

- Cervical, thoracic and lumbar spine: neutral in transition for slight flexion.
- Shoulder: neutral position for hyperextension.
- Elbow: slight flexion in transition to full extension.
- Fist and fingers: neutral position in transition to extension supporting on the ground.
- Hip: flexion.
- Knee: from flexion in transition to extension.
- Ankle: neutral position.

MOVEMENT EXECUTION: sitting on the ball, the practitioner throws his feet upwards, pulling off the ground and resting his hands, replacing the supports.

ACTIVATED MUSCLES: TRUNK: rectus abdominis lower portion, oblique internal and external. UPPER LIMBS: deltoid posterior fibers (rotator cuff) major and minor, rhomboids, trapezius, triceps, anecdotal, wrist extensors. LOWER LIMBS: rectus femoris, iliopsoas, adductors and plantar flexors (isometric); quadriceps (isotonic).

LEVEL AND GOALS:

- Perform movement in the frontal plane;
- Work the postural reactions. (Equilibrium, rectification and straightening);
- Promote elbow flexion of the shoulder and elbow in a closed chain at the end of the movement;
- Promote strengthening of the lower abdominal muscles and open-hip hip flexors at the end of the movement;
- Promote balance and coordination.

UPSIDE DOWN

Fig. 164

MOVEMENTS AND JOINT POSITIONS

- Cervical, Thoracic and Lumbar Column: neutral position in transition for extension.

- Shoulder: left Flexion and right extension. in transition to flexion with bilateral abduction.

- Elbow: flexion can vary for maximum extension.

- Fist and fingers: neutral position in transition for extension by supporting the palms on the ground.

- Hip: transitional flexion for bilateral extension.

- Knee: right flexion and left extension in transition to bilateral extension.

- Ankle: dorsal flexion in transition to plantar flexion

MOVEMENT EXECUTION: sitting on the ball, the practitioner applies a force on the shoulder girdle laterally and downwards, withdrawing the feet from the ground and supporting with the hands on the ground and the lower limbs present in hip and knee flexion. There may be a variation with the whole body in extension and flexed shoulders with the elbow extended.

ACTIVATED MUSCLES: TRUNK: spinal erector, lumbar, paravertebral, abdominal and oblique erector. UPPER LIMBS: rhomboids, anterior serratil, lateral and anterior fiber deltoid, biceps, brachial, coracobrachial, triceps, LOWER LIMBS: gluteus maximus and medius, hamstrings and triceps sural.

LEVEL AND GOALS:

- Movement with a high degree of excursion;
- Movement performed in the oblique plane;
- Develop balance, and weight transfer from LOWER LIMBS to UPPER LIMBS;
- Strengthen extensor muscles of the spine and shoulder girdle;
- Strengthen the musculature of the shoulder and elbow by supporting the body with closed-chain hands.

ANTERIOR DODGE

Fig. 165

MOVEMENTS AND ARTICULAR POSITIONS

- Cervical, Thoracic and Lumbar Spine: flexion.
- Scapular girdle: bilateral abduction.
- Shoulder: right flexion and left horizontal abduction.
- Elbow: right flexion and extension of the left in transition for bilateral flexion.
- Hip: flexion.
- Knee: bilateral flexion.
- Ankle: slight plantar flexion in transition for bilateral dorsal flexion

MOVEMENT EXECUTION: the practitioner sitting on the ball flexes the spine by placing his hands on the ground, descending the body towards the ground.

ACTIVATED MUSCLES: By involving complex movement of the body and multiple joints multiple muscles participate simultaneously (synergism). We will only address a few muscles: TRUNK: Straight abdominal, oblique, lumbar spine erector spine, transvertebral, cervical flexors. UPPER LIMBS: Muscles of the shoulder girdle: rhomboids, medial and inferior trapezius, anterior and lateral deltoid, coracobrachial, infraespinal, triceps anconeus and biceps, brachiaria, extensors of the wrist. LOWER LIMBS: Iliopsoas, ischiostibial, tibialis anterior and fibular third (front leg).

LEVEL AND GOALS:

- Moderate difficulty level;
- Make movement in oblique plane;
- Mobilize the spine joint in flexion-extension with slight rotation and lateral flexion;
- Mobilize the hip and knee joints in flexion-extension and ankle in plantar flexion and dorsal flexion in closed chain;
- Promote elongation of spine extensors during spinal flexion;
- Promote stretching of the extensors of the hip and right knee (front leg);
- Promote activation of the hip and knee flexor and extensor muscles;
- Promote activation of the flexor muscles, extensors, lateral flexors and spinal rotators;
- Promote passive stretching of the flexors of the wrist and the plantar flexors (front foot).

POSTERIOR DODGE

Fig. 166a   Fig. 166b

Movement of extension of the trunk supporting the hand behind the ball

MOVEMENTS AND ARTICULAR POSITIONS

- Cervical, thoracic and lumbar spine: flexion and lateral flexion in transition for extension with slight rotation.
- Scapular girdle: abduction in transition for bilateral adduction.
- Shoulder: right flexion and left horizontal abduction.
- Elbow: right flexion and extension of the left.
- Hip: transitional flexion for slight extension of the right and slight flexion in transition for extension of the left.
- Knee: flexion in transition to mild bilateral extension.
- Ankle: light Dorsal flexion in transition for bilateral plantar flexion.

MOVEMENT EXECUTION: the practitioner sitting on the ball makes a slight extension of the spine by pushing the ball forward by touching the posterior lateral region on the ball, extending the right hip.

ACTIVATED MUSCLES: By involving complex body movement multiple joints and muscles work simultaneously

LEVEL AND GOALS:

- Movement with moderate level of difficulty;
- Make movement in oblique plane;
- Mobilize the spine joint in flexion-extension with slight rotation and lateral flexion;
- Mobilize the hip and knee joints in flexion and extension in plantar flexion and dorsal flexion in closed chain;
- Promote stretching of the abs during extension of the spine;
- Promote stretching of the hip flexors (back leg);
- Promote activation of scapular belt adductor muscles;
- Promote activation of the hip and knee flexor and extensor muscles;
- Promote activation of the plantar and dorsal flexor muscles.

BLESSING

Fig. 167

POSITIONS AND ARTICULAR MOVEMENTS

- Cervical Spine: Slight flexion; Thoracic and Lumbar: transition flexion for slight extension.
- Scapular girdle: abduction in transition for a slight adduction.
- Shoulder: right flexion and left horizontal abduction.
- Elbow: bilateral flexion being the right to a greater degree.
- Hip: from flexion to slight extension of right and flexion to extension of left.
- Knee: flexion for extension of the right and slight flexion for slight extension of the left.
- Ankle: from dorsal flexion to plantar flexion.

MOVEMENT EXECUTION: the practitioner sitting on the ball performs extension of the spine accompanied by a flexion of the right hip with the knee extended, taking the foot forward, the torso facing upwards with the back in the ball.

ACTIVATED MUSCLES: By involving complex body movement multiple muscles and joints work simultaneously.

LEVEL AND GOALS:

- Movement from a basic to moderate level in execution;
- Perform movement in the sagittal plane of the flexed limb in the open front;
- Mobilize the spine joint in flexion-extension;
- Mobilize the hip and knee joints in flexion and ankle flexion in plantar flexion and dorsal flexion;
- Promote strengthening of the abdominals with the raised leg;
- Promote activation of the hip and right knee flexor and extensor muscles;
- Promote strengthening of the hip flexors of the raised leg;
- Promote balance and work postural reactions;
- Promote physical fitness if you perform several times.

HAMMER

Fig. 168

POSITIONS AND ARTICULAR MOVEMENTS

- Cervical Spine: Slight flexion; Thoracic and Lumbar: transition flexion for slight extension.

- Scapular girdle: abduction in transition for a slight adduction.

- Shoulder: direct flexion and left horizontal abduction.

- Elbow bilateral flexion being the right to a greater degree.

- Hip: from flexion to slight abduction with flexion of the right and flexion to slight extension of the left.

- Knee: from flexion to extension of the right and slight left flexion.

- Ankle: from dorsal flexion to plantar flexion.

MOVEMENT EXECUTION: the practitioner sitting on the ball performs extension of the spine accompanied by a flexion and abduction of the right hip with the knee extended with the trunk facing upwards.

ACTIVATED MUSCLES: by involving complex body movement multiple muscles and joints work simultaneously.

LEVEL AND GOALS:

- Movement from a basic to moderate level in execution;
- Perform movement in the ablated plane of the flexed limb in the open chain front;
- Mobilize the spine joint in flexion-extension and slight lateral flexion;
- Mobilize the hip abduction and knee joints in flexion and ankle flexion in plantar flexion and dorsal flexion;
- Promote strengthening of the abdominals with the raised leg;
- Promote activation of the abductors, flexors and extensors of the hip and knee;
- Promote balance and work postural reactions;
- Promote physical fitness when performed several times.

SWEEP

Fig. 169

POSITIONS AND ARTICULAR MOVEMENTS

- Cervical, thoracic and lumbar spine: flexion with lateral flexion in transition for inferior trunk rotation.
- Shoulder: left abduction with right flexion.
- Elbow: extension in transition for slight flexion of the left and flexion of the right.
- Hip: performs a circular movement of the right and flexion of the left.
- Knee: flexion in transition to extension of the right and increase of the flexion of the left.
- Ankle: dorsal flexion in transition for right inversion and increased left plantar flexion.

MOVEMENT EXECUTION: the practitioner sitting on the ball makes a circle-shaped movement with the back foot, touching the lateral side of the left thigh in the ball, performing a rotation of the lower trunk

ACTIVATED MUSCLES: TRUNK: Trapezoid, ecom, platima, supra hyoid and infrahyoid (isometric), oblique, rectus abdominis. UPPER LIMBS: rotator cuff, deltoid, rhomboid bilateral trapezius bilateral. LOWER LIMBS: iliopsoas, rectus femoris, fascia lata, sartorius, pectinium, gracilis in flexion. Upper and middle gluteus, biceps femoris, semitendinosus, semimembranosus, adductor magnus at extension (bipodal), long, short adductor, magno (extended leg) quadriceps (extended leg) iliopsoas and rectus femoris isometric, anterior tibialis).

LEVEL AND GOALS:

- Movement - Moderate Level;
- Perform movement in the oblique plane;
- Mobilize the shoulder joint in flexion-extension;
- Mobilize the spine in rotation and flexion;
- Promote elongation of spinal rotators;
- Mobilize the hip and knee joints in flexion-extension and ankle in plantar flexion and dorsal flexion in closed chain;
- Promote stretching of hip extensors and abductors and extended leg knee extensors;
- Promote activation of the adductor and hip abductor flexor and extensor muscles and knee flexors and extensors;
- Promote activation of the plantar and dorsal flexor muscles;
- Promote balance.

HALF MOON (FROM INSIDE OUT WITH HAND ON THE BALL)

Fig. 170

POSITIONS AND ARTICULAR MOVEMENTS

- Cervical, Thoracic and Lumbar Column: neutral position for slight flexion.
- Scapular girdle: bilateral adduction.
- Shoulder: extension with slight abduction.
- Elbow: flexion.
- Handle: extension supported on the ball.
- Hip: from flexion with adduction to complete abduction in right-hand and right-hand flexion.
- Knee: from flexion to extension of the right and flexion of the left.
- Ankle: neutral position.

MOVEMENT EXECUTION: the practitioner sitting on the ball performs a combined movement of flexion, adduction and abduction of the hip as an extended knee, making a circular movement with the foot, raised from the inside out.

ACTIVATED MUSCLES: by involving complex body movement where multiple muscles and joints work simultaneously. TRUNK:

Abdominal rectum, oblique, focusing only on the uterus that elevates LOWER LIMBS: (iliopsoas, rectus femoris, pectineum, tensor from fascia to can, vast medial, intermediate and lateral, adductors and abductors, anterior tibial, fibular third.

LEVEL AND GOALS:

- Movement with a high level in execution.
- Perform movement in the oblique plane;
- Mobilize the hip joints in circumference (raised leg) and knee flexion-extension and ankle in plantar flexion and dorsal flexion;
- Promote strengthening of the abs with a raised leg;
- Promote activation of the right hip flexor, adductor and abductor muscles;
- Promote activation of the knee and ankle flexor and extensor muscles;
- Work the postural reactions (balance, straightening and rectification);
- Work balance and coordination;
- Work resistance when run several times.

HALF MOON (FROM INSIDE OUT WITH HAND ON THE GROUND)

Fig. 171

POSITIONS AND ARTICULAR MOVEMENTS

- Cervical column: neutral position; Thoracic and Lumbar: neutral position or with slight flexion in transition for a slight extension.

- Shoulder girdle: abduction in transition for mild adduction.

- Shoulder: right flexion, transitional abduction to left extension.

- Pelvic girdle: slight retroversion.

- Hip: transitional flexion for extension of the raised leg and the other remains in flexion.

- Knee: flexion in transition for extension of the raised leg, the other remains in flexion.

- Ankle: dorsal flexion in transition to plantar flexion, the other foot remains neutral.

MOVEMENT EXECUTION: the practitioner sitting on the ball performs a hip flexion and abduction and knee extension, making a circular movement with the foot raised from the inside out.

ACTIVATED MUSCLES: UPPER LIMBS: the posterior and posterior deltoid, rhomboids, medial trapezius bilateral, pectoralis major (of the hand supported on the ground). LOWER LIMBS:

iliopsoas, rectus femoris, fascia lata, sartorius, in the flexion. Gluteus maximus and medius, biceps femoris, semitendinosus, semimembranosus, adductor magnus in extension (bipodal), iliopsoas and rectus femoris isometric (unipodal).

LEVEL AND GOALS:

- Moderate Level;
- Perform movement in oblique plane;
- Mobilize the shoulder joint in flexion-extension;
- Mobilize hip, abduction, flexion and knee joints in flexion and ankle in plantar flexion and dorsal flexion in closed chain;
- Promote activation of the flexor and extensor muscles and abductors of the hip and flexors and extensors of the knee;
- Promote balance and coordination;
- Work resistance when performed several times.

ARROW

Fig. 172

POSITIONS AND ARTICULAR MOVEMENTS

- Cervical, thoracic and lumbar spine: neutral position in transition for a slight extension with lateral flexion.

- Shoulder: abduction and adduction.

- Elbow: extension in transition for flexion.

- Wrist: extension movement to the neutral position of the right and neutral position of the left.

- Hip: 90° transitional flexion for slight extension of the lower limbs (from above) and / or Bilateral.

- Knee: from flexion to extension (with the variation one of knees is flexed).

- Ankle: dorsal flexion for plantar flexion.

MOVEMENT EXECUTION: the practitioner sitting on the ball makes a diagonal movement, withdrawing both feet and extending one or both knees with one of the forearms as support on the ground.

ACTIVATED MUSCLES: complex movements that make use of much of the body's muscles. Upper and lower extremity trapezius, upper and lower extremity trapezius, eosinopharyngeal, midline, suprahyoid and infrahyoid (isometric), paravertebral, oblique interspinhais, lumbar quadrate, rectus abdominis, UPPER LIMBS:

posterior and lateral deltoid, rhomboids, bilateral trapezius, rotator cuff, coracobrachial, triceps, anchored arm resting on the ground. LOWER LIMBS: iliopsoas, rectus femoris, tensor of fascia lata, sartorius, pectinium, gracilis in flexion. Upper and middle gluteus, biceps femoris, semitendinosus, semimembranosus, adductor magnus, short and long in extension).

LEVEL AND GOALS:

- Perform sagging in the sagittal plane;
- Promote activation and strengthening of the arm muscles when supported on the ground;
- Promote activation and strengthening of the trunk muscles and hip adductors;
- Promote activation of the hip and knee flexor and extensor muscles;
- Promote activation of the plantar and dorsal flexor muscles;
- Promote balance and coordination.

COMPASS

Fig. 173

POSITIONS AND ARTICULAR MOVEMENTS

- Cervical, thoracic and lumbar spine: from the neutral position in transition to a slight flexion.

- Hip: bilateral abduction in transition for slight flexion with abduction.

- Knee: flexion in transition for extension of the rotating leg.

- Ankle: plantar flexion in transition for right dorsal flexion.

- Fingers: extension.

MOVEMENT EXECUTION: the practitioner with the left side of the trunk on the ball and the left hand as support in the ground, performs an abduction of the right leg, with extension of the knee, turning the trunk on the ball to the left supporting the right hand in the ground.

ACTIVATED MUSCLES: BODY: Oblique, lumbar square, rectus abdominis, spine and interspinal erections. UPPER LIMBS: rotator cuff, deltoid, pectoralis major, rhomboids, bilateral trapezius bilateral. LOWER LIMBS: Gluteus medius, minimus, and maximus, iliopsoas, rectus femoris, fascia, sartorius, pectinium of the leg above.

LEVEL AND GOALS:

- Perform movement in the oblique plane;
- Mobilizes the hip joint in abduction;
- Promote stretching of the knee flexors in the final position;
- Promote activation and strengthening of the lateral flexor muscles of the trunk above the ball;
- Promote activation of the hip abductor muscles;
- Promote balance and coordination.

AÚ – HAND STOP

Fig. 174

POSITIONS AND ARTICULAR MOVEMENTS

- Cervical, Thoracic and Lumbar Column: position of lateral flexion in transition for flexion ending with an extension of the lumbar.

- Shoulder: adduction of the left in transition for abduction; Flexion of right in transition for abduction.

- Elbow: bilateral flexion.

- Hip: bilateral flexion.

- Knee: right flexion and extension of the left in transition for extension and ending for bilateral flexion.

- Ankle: from dorsal flexion in transition to plantar flexion.

MOVEMENT EXECUTION: the practitioner with the left side of the trunk on the ball makes a lateral flexion of the column to the left, removing the foot that is behind and turning the body on the ball touching the region of the back and the neck in the ball. Passing the left foot over the other foot, leaning on the same line as the right foot, transferring the weight of the body to the hand and to the ball taking the feet off the ground, staying in the handstand.

COMPLEX MOVEMENT: Involving Multiple Muscles of the upper and lower limb spine.

LEVEL AND GOALS:

- Perform movement in the oblique plane;
- Mobilize the spine joint in lateral flexion and flexion;
- Mobilize the hip and knee joints in flexo-extension and abduction and ankle in plantar flexion and dorsal flexion in closed chain;
- Promote stretching of the spine and hip extensors when both feet are resting on the ground;
- Promote activation of the trunk flexor and extensor muscles;
- Promotes activation and strengthening of the shoulder girdle muscles at the handstand;
- Promote balance;
- Increase intracranial pressure and venous return.

COMPLETE HAND STOP

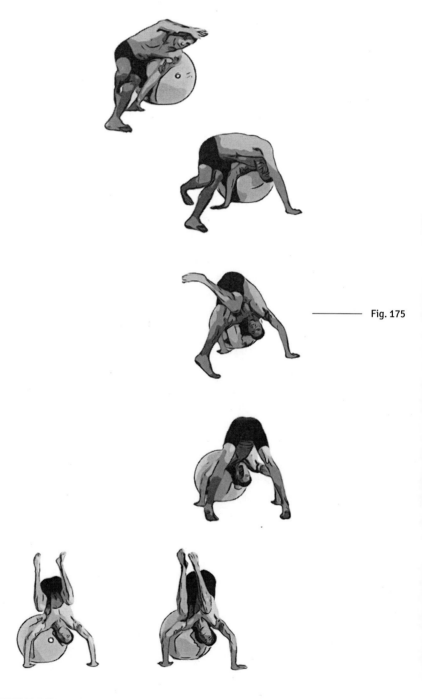

Fig. 175

BACK EDUCATIONAL EXERCISES

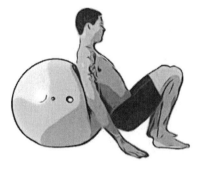

The next exercises illustrated below are made in the primary position of back in which the starting position will always have as base of support, the feet, sometimes the hands and the ball. The point of contact between the body and the ball will be the torso. It is always good to observe and analyze these exercises to be applied correctly, because depending on the patient, student and practitioner may have a contraindication. It is necessary to be identified by each professional in the field. Most of these exercises present a kinesiological analysis containing information such as: the achievement of movement, positions and joint movements, activated muscles and objectives. Everything for a better reader comprehension.

STRETCHING THE ABDOMEN

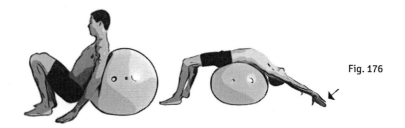

Fig. 176

POSITIONS AND ARTICULAR MOVEMENTS

- Cervical, thoracic and lumbar spine: from the neutral position to hyperextension.
- Shoulder girdle: neutral position for upward rotation.
- Shoulder: from extension to 180° flexion and bilateral external rotation.
- Elbow: from flexion to extension with pronation.
- Hip: from 90° flexion to full extension.
- Knee: from flexion to extension.
- Ankle: from dorsal flexion to plantar flexion.

MOVEMENT EXECUTION: the practitioner with the back on the ball carries out an extension and flexion of the hip and the knee, moving the ball forward and backward abducting and fully adducting the upper limbs accompanied by a hyperextension of the spine.

ACTIVATED MUSCLES: BODY: upper trapezius, splenius of the head and neck, interspinal spine erectors. UPPER LIMBS: deltoid, coracobrachial and pectoralis major in flexion of 180° biceps brachii, brachial. LOWER LIMBS: iliopsoas, rectus femoris, tensor of fascia lata, sartorius, pectinium, gracilis in flexion. Maximus medius and minimus gluteus, biceps femoris, semitendinosus, semimembranosus, adductor magnus in extension.

LEVEL AND GOALS:

- Basic Level;
- Performing sagging in the sagittal plane;
- Mobilize the column from the neutral position to extension;
- Mobilize the articulations of the spine and hip and knee and flexion-extension and ankle in plantar flexion and dorsal flexion;
- Promote elongation of the trunk flexors (abdominals);
- Promote activation of the flexor and extensor muscles of the hip and knee in a closed chain.

COMPLETE STRETCHING

Fig. 177

POSITIONS AND ARTICULAR MOVEMENTS

- Cervical, thoracic and lumbar spine: neutral position in transition to extension.

- Shoulder: extension in transition for flexion of 180 cranes with external rotation.

- Elbow: flexion in transition for extension with pronation.

- Hip: 90° transitional flexion for full extension or flexion with raised limb (variation).

- Knee: flexion in transition to full extension.

- Ankle: dorsal flexion in transition to plantar flexion.

MOVEMENT EXECUTION: the practitioner with the back on the ball performs a hip and knee extension, moving the ball backwards fully abducting the upper limbs accompanied by a hyperextension of the spine, ending with a hip flexion and extension of the knee of the leg high.

ACTIVATED MUSCLES: TRUNK: cervical trapezius superior, splenius of the head and neck. UPPER LIMBS: Deltoid, coracobrachial in flexion of 180°, biceps brachii, brachial. LOWER LIMBS: gluteus maximus, medial posterior hamstring fibers, adductors, iliopsoas, rectus femoris, vastus, soleus, gastrognemius of the raised leg.

LEVEL AND GOALS:

- Moderate movement;
- Performing sagging in the sagittal plane;
- Mobilize the spine, hip and knee joints in flexion and ankle flexion in plantar flexion and dorsal flexion;
- Mobilizes the speaker from the neutral position to extension;
- Promote elongation of the anterior trunk and hip flexors;
- Promote activation of the hip and knee flexor and extensor muscles;
- Promote balance work.

TRUNK ROTATIONAL BALANCE

Fig. 178

POSITIONS AND ARTICULAR MOVEMENTS

- Cervical, thoracic and lumbar spine: slight flexion accompanied by rotation.

- Shoulder: slight adduction with bilateral flexion.

- Elbow: bilateral flexion.

- Fist and fingers: neutral.

- Hip: adduction in transition for abduction alternately.

- Knee: gentle flexion with alternating internal and external rotation rotation.

- Ankle: neutral.

MOVEMENT EXECUTION: the practitioner with the back on the ball makes a slight rotation of the trunk, rolling the ball to one side and the other, the upper limbs adducted horizontally with elbow flexion, the lower limbs perform a slight adduction and alternating abduction.

ACTIVATED MUSCLES: Cervical: sternocleidomastoid, platysma, hyoid complex, TRUNK: rectus abdominis, internal and external oblique, spine and interspinal erectors. UPPER LIMBS:

Deltoid, pectoralis major, coracobrachial, biceps brachii and brachial bilateral (isometric) LOWER LIMBS: iliopsoas, rectus femoris, adductor magnus, long, short, pectin of the limb in adduction and gluteus medius, tensor of the fascia to the can of the abducting limb.

LEVEL AND GOALS:

- Perform movement in the transverse plane;
- Mobilize the spine in flexion and rotation.
- Promote strengthening of the abs and rotators.
- Promote activation of adductor and abductor muscles of the hip and knee in a closed chain.
- Promote balance and coordination.

ROTATIONAL TRUNK SWING WITH UPPER LIMBS HORIZONTALLY ADMITTED

Fig. 179

POSITIONS AND ARTICULAR MOVEMENTS

- Cervical, thoracic and lumbar spine: slight flexion accompanied by rotation.
- Shoulder: horizontal adduction with mild bilateral flexion.
- Elbow: bilateral extension.
- Fist and fingers: neutral.
- Hip: adduction in transition for abduction alternately.
- Knee: flexion, internal and external rotation alternately.
- Ankle: neutral.

MOVEMENT EXECUTION: the practitioner with the back in the ball realizes a total rotation of the trunk, the superior members adducted horizontally with extension of the elbow and palm of the united hands.

MUSCLES ACTIVATED: TRUMP: platysma, hyoid complex, abdominal rectus, internal and external oblique. UPPER LIMBS: deltoid, Pectoralis major, large dorsal, anterior serratil, coracobrachial, biceps brachii, triceps and anechoic (isometric). LOWER LIMBS:

iliopsoas, rectum femoral, adductor magnus, long, short, pectin of the limb in adduction and gluteus medius, tensor of the fascia to the can of the limb in abduction.

LEVEL AND GOALS:

- Basic movement;
- Perform movement in the transverse plane;
- Mobilizes the spine in slight flexion and rotation;
- Promote strengthening of the abs and rotators;
- Promote activation of the adductor muscles of the shoulder in a closed chain;
- Promote activation of adductor and abductor muscles of the hip in a closed chain;
- Promote balance.

ROTATIONAL SWING WITH TRUNK FLEXION

Fig. 180

ARTICULAR MOTIONS AND MOVEMENTS

- Cervical, thoracic and lumbar spine: neutral position in transition for flexion accompanied by rotation.
- Scapular girdle: neutral position in transition to Abduction.
- Shoulder: slight bilateral flexion.
- Elbow: bilateral flexion.
- Fist and fingers: neutral or slight flexion.
- Hip: extension in transition for flexion.
- Knee: mild flex with slight internal and external rotation alternately for each limb.
- Ankle: neutral.

MOVEMENT EXECUTION: the practitioner with the back in the ball performs a trunk flexion accompanied by rotation, the flexed upper limbs with flexion of the elbow, the lower limbs flex and light extension of hip and knee.

ACTIVATED MUSCLES: Cervical: sternocleidomastoid, platysma, hyoid complex. TRUNK: rectus abdominis, internal and external oblique. UPPER LIMBS: deltoid, pectoralis major, coracobrachial, biceps brachii, brachial (isometric). LOWER LIMBS: iliopsoas, rectus femoris, adductor magnus, long, short, pectin (limb in adduction) and gluteus medius, tensor of the fascia (limb in abduction).

LEVEL AND GOALS:

- Basic Level;
- Perform movement in the oblique plane;
- Mobilize the spine in flexion and rotation;
- Promote strengthening of the abs and spinal column;
- Promote activation of the flexor, adductor and abductor muscles of the hip and knee in a closed chain;
- Promote balance and coordination.

DIAGONAL STRETCHING

Fig. 181

POSITIONS AND ARTICULAR MOVEMENTS

- Cervical, thoracic and lumbar spine: neutral position in transition for lateral flexion with extension and rotation.

- Shoulder: movement leaves adduction in transition to flexion.

- Elbow: slight flexion in transition to extension of the supported member in the ground.

- Wrist and fingers: neutral in transition for extension of supported hand.

- Hip: flexion in transition to extension.

- Knee: flexion in transition to extension.

- Ankle: neutral in transition for eversion and alternate inversion.

MOVEMENT EXECUTION: starting from the primary position of the back and one of the upper limbs in adduction, the practitioner performs extension of the hip and knee accompanied by a rotation of the trunk to the side of the upper limb adduced. The same upper limb touches the ground.

ACTIVATED MUSCLES: TRUNK: oblique, spinal erector, lumbar, interspinal, multifidus, dorsal, semispinal and rotator. LOWER LIMBS: gluteus maximus, vastus, rectus femoris, hamstrings (proximal portion) and adductors.

LEVEL AND GOALS:

- Perform movement in the oblique plane;
- Mobilize the column from the neutral position in transition to extension, lateral bending and rotation;
- Mobilize the hip and knee joints in flexo-extension;
- Promote elongation of obliques;
- Promote activation of the flexor and extensor muscles of the hip and knee in a closed chain.

BRIDGE

Fig. 182

POSITIONS AND ARTICULAR MOVEMENTS

- • Cervical, thoracic and lumbar spine: extension in transition for hyperextension of the lower trunk.

- Scapular Waist: neutral position in transition for upward rotation.

- Shoulder: extension in transition for bilateral flexion.

- Elbow: slight flexion in transition to extension with slight bilateral supination.

- Handle and fingers: movement exits from extension to neutral position.

- Hip: adduction movement with flexion in transition for extension.

- Knee: bending in transition to slight extension.

- Ankle: neutral position.

MOVEMENT EXECUTION: the practitioner with the back (region of the cervical and upper back) in the ball performs an extension of the inferior trunk, hip and knee moving away the gluteal of the ground and aligning it in the height of the knee. It ends with a full shoulder flexion.

ACTIVATED MUSCLES: TRUNK: spinal erector, lumbar, interspinal, multifidus, dorsal and semispinal. UPPER LIMBS: deltoid, coracobrachial, biceps brachii, triceps and ancneum. LOWER LIMBS:

gluteus maximus, medium (posterior portion), adductor magno, long, short, biceps (long portion), semitendinosus and semimembranosus.

LEVEL AND GOALS:

- Perform movement in the sagittal plane;
- Work the balance;
- Mobilize inferior trunk in flexo-extension;
- Promote strengthening of spine extensors and hip extensors;
- Promote open flexion of the shoulder flexor muscles;
- Promote activation of the adductor and extensor muscles of the hip and flexors and extensors of the knee in a closed chain.

DEPRESSION AND ESCAPULAR LIFT

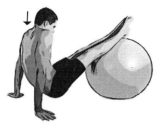

Fig. 183

POSITIONS AND ARTICULAR MOVEMENTS

- Cervical, thoracic and lumbar spine: slight flexion.
- Scapular Waist: elevation in transition to depression.
- Shoulder: bilateral extension.
- Elbow: bilateral extension.
- Wrist and fingers: extension.
- Hip: adduction with flexion.
- Knee: extension.
- Ankle: plantar flexion.

MOVEMENT EXECUTION: With the back of the leg on the ball and the hand on the ground the practitioner pushes his hand against the ground, raises the trunk and depresses the shoulder girdle keeping the elbow extended throughout the movement.

ACTIVATED MUSCLES: TRUNK: erector spines, rectus abdominis and obliques. UPPER LIMBS: scapula lift, trapezius medial and inferior fibers, deltoid (posterior portion), major and minor pectoralis, anterior serratus, rotator cuff, triceps, anecdotal and wrist extensors. LOWER LIMBS: vastus, rectus femoris, gluteus medius (anterior portion), iliopsoas, adductor magno, long, short, biceps (long portion), semitendinosus and semimembranosus.

LEVEL AND GOALS:

- Perform movement in the sagittal plane;
- Work the balance;
- Mobilize shoulder girdle in depression and elevation;
- Promote strengthening of elbow extensors symmetrically;
- Promote activation of the depressor muscles and scapula elevators in a closed chain;
- Promote activation of the adductor muscles of the hip;
- Promote activation of the abdominal muscles to stabilize the trunk and the ball slide sideways.

BALLOON

This movement requires a mastery and an optimal balance on the ball. With the lateral and posterior region of the trunk in direct contact with the ball, the practitioner throws the legs over the ball and can be made with the knees bent or extended as shown in the central figure. This movement is performed in the oblique plane and involves multiple joints. It develops balance, coordination of movement between axial skeleton with the appendicular, self-confidence with the ball and allows weight transfer between the feet and the hands used in the performances with the dance and the capoeira.

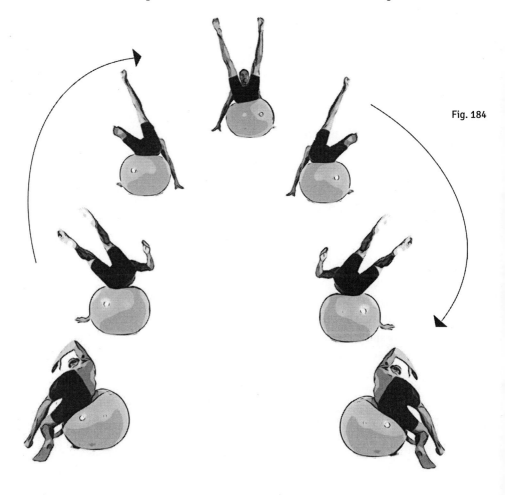

Fig. 184

CHEST EDUCATION

The exercises illustrated below are made in the primary chest position. The initial position will always have as a base of support the hands and the ball and the contact of the TRUNK in the ball will be the chest and sometimes the abdomen. Some of these exercises were extracted from the literature and referred to as conventional, while other exercises are part of the SAMIBALL methodology and were created from inspiring sources. It is always good to observe and analyze these exercises to be applied correctly, because depending on the patient, student and practitioner there may be contraindication. It is necessary to be identified by each professional in the area. Most of these exercises present a kinesiological analysis containing information such as: the achievement of movement, positions and joint movements, activated muscles and goals. All to help the reader's understanding.

BASIC POINTS

Some observations of chest position

Ideal joint positions:

Fig. 185

- 0° of hip.
- 0° of knee.
- Ankle in neutral position.
- Gravitational center in an ideal position.
- Curvatures of the present column.

Position with angular changes of joints:

Fig. 186

- Angle of 30° to 40° of the hip.
- More inflated ball.
- Highest gravitational center.
- Ankle in plantar flexion.
- Rectification of the curvature of the thoracic and lumbar spin.

SUPPORTED PLANK

Fig. 187

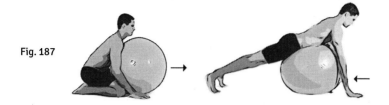

POSITIONS AND ARTICULAR MOVEMENTS

- Cervical, thoracic and lumbar spine: slight flexion in transition to neutral extension.

- Shoulder: slight flexion in flexion transition of ninety degrees.

- Elbow: flexion in transition to extension.

- Wrist and fingers: from the neutral position in transition to extension.

- Hip: flexion in transition to extension.

- Knee: Flexion in transition to extension.

- Ankle: from plantar flexion in transition to neutral position.

MOVEMENT EXECUTION: the practitioner performs a full extension of the lower limbs by pushing the ball forward with hand support on the ground and shoulder flexion. Returns the movement with a knee and hip flexion by rolling the ball back by sitting on the heel.

ACTIVATED MUSCLES: TRUNK: erector spines and upper trapezius. UPPER LIMBS: anterior deltoid, biceps (long portion), pectoralis major and minor, serratus anterior, trapezius medium fibers, triceps, coracobrachial, large dorsal, rotator cuff. LOWER LIMBS: gluteus, quadriceps and triceps sural.

LEVEL AND GOALS:

- Basic level;
- Perform movement in the sagittal plane;
- Mobilize the column from the neutral position to extension;
- Mobilize the hip and knee joints in flexo-extension;
- Promote activation of the flexor and extensor muscles of the hip and knee in a closed chain;
- Promote activation of the shoulder girdle and shoulder muscles;
- Work the strength of the diaphragm muscle generated by the resistance in the ball over the abdomen.

HYPEREXTENSION OF THE UPPER TRUNK SUPPORTING THE BALL

Fig. 188

POSITIONS AND ARTICULAR MOVEMENTS

- Cervical, thoracic and lumbar spine: neutral position in transition for hyperextension.
- Shoulder: flexion in transition to extension.
- Elbow: extension in transition for slight flexion.
- Wrist and fingers: extension resting on the ground for the ball.
- Hip: extension in transition for hyperextension.
- Knee: extension.
- Ankle: neutral in transition to plantar flexion.

MOVEMENT EXECUTION: Practicing with the abdomen and chest on the ball removes the hand of the ground, extends the column and supports the hands in the ball.

ACTIVATED MUSCLES: TRUNK: erector spines, lumbar square and upper trapezius. UPPER LIMBS: anterior deltoid, biceps (long portion), pectoralis major and minor, serratus anterior, trapezius medium fibers, triceps, coracobrachial, large dorsal, rotator cuff. LOWER LIMBS: glutes, hamstrings (proximal portion), quadriceps and triceps sural.

LEVEL AND GOALS:

- Perform movement in the sagittal plane;
- Mobilize the column from the neutral position to extension;
- Mobilize the scapular waist from adduction abduction;
- Work proprioception of the shoulder girdle, shoulder, elbow and wrist;
- Promote activation of the extensor muscles of the spine;
- Work the balance;
- Promote activation of the adductor and extensor muscles of the shoulder.

PLANK WITH FOREARM SUPPORT ON THE BALL

Fig. 189

POSITIONS AND ARTICULAR MOVEMENTS

- Cervical, thoracic and lumbar spine: neutral position in transition for mild flexion.
- Scapular girdle: adduction in transition for abduction.
- Shoulder: neutral extension in transition for flexion.
- Elbow: bilateral flexion in transition for pronation and flexion.
- Wrist and fingers: neutral position in transition for mild bilateral flexion.
- Hip: bilateral extension.
- Knee: bilateral extension.
- Ankle: neutral position.

MOVEMENT EXECUTION: the practitioner with the abdomen and hands in contact with the ball disengages them, supports the forearm and performs a slight flexion of the spine.

ACTIVATED MUSCLES: TRUNK: rectus abdominis, interspinhais, transverse abdomen, spine erectors, upper and middle trapezius and rhomboids. UPPER LIMBS: medial trapezius, rhomboids, large dorsal, deltoid (anterior portion), rotator cuff, coracobrachial, triceps and anecdotal. LOWER LIMBS: gluteus maximus, quadriceps (isometry) and adductors.

LEVEL AND GOALS:

- Perform movement in the sagittal plane;
- Activate isometrically the muscles of the shoulder girdle, shoulder and spine;
- Promote activation of the spinal flexor muscles;
- Working proprioception of the shoulder girdle and shoulder joint;
- Promote activation of lateral trunk muscles (not to let the ball roll sideways);
- Promote balance;
- Promote isometric strengthening of the shoulder girdle.

SUPERIOR TRUNK EXTENSION WITH HANDS BEHIND THE HEAD

Fig. 190

POSITIONS AND ARTICULAR MOVEMENTS

- Cervical, thoracic and lumbar spine: neutral position in transition to hyperextension.
- Shoulder: horizontal abduction.
- Elbow: flexion.
- Wrist and fingers: neutral extension.
- Hip: extension.
- Knee: extension.
- Ankle: neutral position.

MOVEMENT EXECUTION: the practitioner with the abdomen on the ball and the hands intertwined behind the head accomplishes a hyperextension of the superior trunk.

ACTIVATED MUSCLES: TRUNK: erector spine, lumbar square UPPER LIMBS: horizontal abductors, rhomboids, medial and minor trapezoid. LOWER LIMBS: gluteus maximus and quadriceps (isometry).

LEVEL AND GOALS:

- Basic level;
- Perform movement in the sagittal plane;
- Mobilize the column from the neutral position to extension;
- Isometric activation of the shoulder and shoulder girdle muscles;
- Promote activation and strengthening of the extensor muscles of the spine;
- Work balance;
- Promote activation of lateral trunk muscles (not to let the ball roll sideways).

ALTERNATE LIFTING OF LIMBS

Fig. 191

POSITIONS AND ARTICULAR MOVEMENTS

- Cervical column: neutral. Thoracic and Lumbar: neutral position for a slight extension.

- Shoulder: 180º bending at just one shoulder, alternating limbs.

- Wrist and fingers: from the extension with the hand resting on the ground in transition to the neutral position when raising the arm.

- Hip: position of slight flexion in transition to the extension position of the limb above.

- Knee: slight flexion of the raised leg.

- Ankle: plantar flexion in transition for dorsal flexion of the raised limb

MOVEMENT EXECUTION: the practitioner removes the support of the members in the soil alternately with the contralateral upper limb.

ACTIVATED MUSCLES: TRUNK: spine erector and lumbar spine (raised lower limb). UPPER LIMBS: deltoid, coracobrachial, biceps long portion, pectoralis major, anterior serratus and trapezius medial fibers (upper limb elevated) LOWER LIMBS: gluteus, hamstrings and triceps sural (lower limb raised).

LEVEL AND GOALS:

- Basic level;
- Perform movement in the sagittal plane;
- Perform weight transfer on the limbs alternately;
- Promote activation of the shoulder, spine and hip muscles;
- Promote balance and coordination;
- Promote alignment of the spine;
- Mobilize and strengthen (isometry) the shoulders and hips in flexion-extension.

DOG LOOKING DOWN

Fig. 192

POSITIONS AND ARTICULAR MOVEMENTS

- Cervical, thoracic and lumbar spine: neutral position in transition for slight flexion only the cervical presents in slight extension.

- Scapular girdle: abduction movement in transition for upward rotation.

- Shoulder: 90° flexion in transition for 180° flexion.

- Elbow: extension.

- Wrist and fingers: bilateral extension.

- Hip: extension movement in transition for flexion.

- Knee: bilateral extension.

- Ankle: neutral position in transition for dorsiflexion.

MOVEMENT EXECUTION: the practitioner with the anterior region of the trunk leaning against the ball performs a shoulder flexion pushing the ball backwards and raises the hip without losing contact with the ball.

ACTIVATED MUSCLES: TRUNK: transverse abdomen, rectus abdominis, spinal erectors, intertransversal, and paravertebral. UPPER LIMBS: rotator cuff, rhomboids, trapezius, deltoid, coracobrachial, triceps, anecdotal and wrist extensors. LOWER LIMBS: iliopsoas, vastus, rectus femoris and tibialis anterior.

LEVEL AND GOALS:

- Basic level;
- Perform movement in the sagittal plane;
- Promote stretching of the posterior musculature of the lower limbs;
- Mobilize the hip in flexo-extension;
- Mobilize the ankle in dorsal and plantar flexion;
- Mobilize the shoulder in flexo-extension and the shoulder girdle in rotation upwards;
- Promote proprioception of the shoulder joint;
- Move the members in closed kinetic chain.

ALTERNATE BALANCE

Fig. 193

POSITIONS AND ARTICULAR MOVEMENTS

- Cervical, thoracic and lumbar spine: neutral position.
- Shoulder: flexion with abduction.
- Elbow: flexion.
- Wrist and fingers: extension.
- Hip: transition flexion for slight extension.
- Knee: bending in transition to slight extension.
- Ankle: movement of dorsal flexion in transition to plantar flexion.

MOVEMENT EXECUTION: the practitioner pushes the TRUNK forward, withdraws the feet from the ground keeping the hip on top of the ball and rests the hands on the ground stopping the movement with the upper limbs. Then it returns to the starting position.

ACTIVATED MUSCLES: TRUNK: spine erector, lumbar square and paravertebral. UPPER LIMBS: deltoid, pectoralis major, serratus anterior, rhomboids, medial and superior trapezius and triceps. LOWER LIMBS: gluteus maximus, hamstrings, soleus and gastrocnemius.

LEVEL AND GOALS:

- Basic level;
- Practice weight transfer by alternating the support of the hands with the feet;
- Activate and strengthen the shoulder girdle and shoulder muscles;
- Work the balance;
- Working the proprioception of upper limbs.

SHOULDER TO PLANK TRANSFERENCE

Fig. 194

POSITIONS AND ARTICULAR MOVEMENTS

- Cervical, thoracic and lumbar spine: slight flexion in transition to extension.
- Shoulder: extension in transition for flexion.
- Elbow: flexion in transition to extension.
- Wrist and fingers: slight flexion in transition to extension.
- Hip: flexion in transition to extension.
- Knee: flexion in transition to extension.
- Ankle: dorsal flexion in transition to plantar flexion.

MOVEMENT EXECUTION: the practitioner pushes the trunk forward, withdraws the feet from the ground with the leg above the ball, upright trunk and support of the hands on the ground stopping the movement. Returns the starting position with a push of the upper limbs back.

ACTIVATED MUSCLES: TRUNK: spine erector, lumbar, paravertebral and transverse abdomen. UPPER LIMBS: deltoid, pectoralis major, serratus anterior, rhomboids, medial and superior trapezius and triceps. LOWER LIMBS: gluteus maximus, hamstrings, soleus and gastrocnemius.

LEVEL AND GOALS:

- Basic to moderate level;
- Practice weight transfer by alternating hands and feet;
- Strengthen the triceps brachii and other muscles of the shoulder girdle in the closed chain;
- Work balance;
- Activate and strengthen the muscles of the abdomen, posterior trunk, and hip extensors

TRUNK PARTIAL ROTATION

Fig. 195

POSITIONS AND ARTICULAR MOVEMENTS

- Cervical, thoracic and lumbar spine: from the neutral position in transition to rotation.

- Shoulder: adduction movement in transition to abduction (alternating).

- Elbow: bilateral extension.

- Wrist and fingers: bilateral extension.

- Hip: bilateral extension.

- Knee: bilateral extension.

- Ankle: neutral with finger support.

MOVEMENT EXECUTION: the practitioner performs a rotation of the trunk with the thorax resting on the ball.

ACTIVATED MUSCLES: TRUNK: internal and external oblique and spinal rotators. UPPER LIMBS: pectoralis major, deltoid and coracobrachial.

LEVEL AND GOALS:

- Basic level;
- Perform the movement in the transverse plane;
- Mobilize the spine in rotation;
- Mobilize the shoulder in horizontal adduction and horizontal abduction;
- Perform elongation of the elbow flexors and wrist flexors;
- Activate the rotator muscles of the trunk;
- Promote proprioception of the shoulder joint.

TOTAL ROTATION OF THE TRUNK TAKING ONE OF THE UPPER LIMBS OFF THE GROUND (VARIATION)

Fig. 196

POSITIONS AND ARTICULAR MOVEMENTS

- Cervical, thoracic and lumbar spine: neutral in transition to rotation.
- Shoulder: horizontal adduction in transition for horizontal abduction.
- Elbow: extension.
- Wrist and fingers: extension.
- Hip: extension.
- Knee: extension.
- Ankle: neutral.

MOVEMENT EXECUTION: the practitioner performs a rotation of the trunk, with the thorax resting on the ball taking the hand off the ground and rolling the ball to the same side of the rotation.

ACTIVATED MUSCLES: TRUNK: internal and external oblique, spinal rotators. UPPER LIMBS: pectoralis major, deltoid, coracobrachial, rhomboids, trapezius fibers of the upper limb.

LEVEL AND GOALS:

- Basic Level;
- Perform movement in the transverse plane.
- Mobilize the spine in rotation.
- Activate the lateral muscles of the trunk and the paravertebrae.
- Promote rotator muscle stretching.
- Promote shoulder mobilization and scapular abduction waist for horizontal adduction and retraction and abduction respectively.
- Promotes stretching of the pectoralis major and flexors of the elbow and wrist.
- Work balance.
- Working shoulder proprioception.

ABDOMINAL SITTING ON THE HEELS

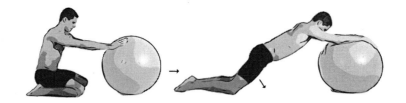

Fig. 197

POSITIONS AND ARTICULAR MOVEMENTS

- Cervical, Thoracic and Lumbar Column: neutral in transition for slight extension.

- Shoulder girdle: neutral in transition for upward rotation.

- Shoulder: 90° flexion in flexion transition of approximately 170° degrees.

- Elbow: extension in transition for slight flexion.

- Wrist and fingers: extension in transition to light bending position.

- Hip: flexion in transition to an extension.

- Knee: full flexion in transition to slight extension.

- Ankle: plantar flexion.

MOVEMENT EXECUTION: the practitioner seated on the heels, performs a hip extension by pushing the ball forward, resting the forearm on the ball. Returns by bringing the ball with the concentric force of the abdomen.

ACTIVATED MUSCLES: TRUNK: Abdominal rectum, internal and external oblique. UPPER LIMBS: Rhomboids, Large dorsal pectoralis major, deltoid, coracobrachial, rhomboids, trapezius fibers of the limb above.

LEVEL AND GOALS:

- Moderate Level;
- Perform movement in the sagittal plane.
- Mobilize the lumbar spine in flexo-extension.
- Activate and strengthen the abdomen and trunk muscles.
- Promote stretching of the extensor muscles of the shoulder.
- Promote mobilization of the shoulder girdle from rotating upwards.

HYPEREXTENSION OF LOWER TRUNK

Fig. 198

POSITIONS AND ARTICULAR MOVEMENTS

- Cervical, thoracic and lumbar spine: neutral for mild hyperextension of lower torso
- Shoulder: transition flexion for horizontal abduction
- Elbow: extension in transition for flexion
- Wrist and fingers: extension
- Hip: light flexion in transition for alternating extension of the members in adduction
- Knee: extension.
- Ankle: neutral position in transition for plantar flexion

MOVEMENT EXECUTION: the practitioner performs an alternating hip extension, removing one foot from the floor and then the other, transferring the support to the upper limbs, then does an abduction of the shoulder with flexion of the elbow pushing the feet upwards.

ACTIVATED MUSCLES: TRUNK: Cervical: Upper trapezius, splenius of the head and neck, semi-spinal of the head and neck, head and neck erectors. The thoracic and lumbar region: Erectors of the lumbar spine, lumbar quadrate, multifidus, paravertebral. UPPER LIMBS: anterior serratus, trapezius, greater peirotal, anterior deltoid, coracobrachial, rhomboids, trapezius fibers, triceps and anchovy. LOWER LIMBS: Hamstrings, gluteus maximus (isotonic), long adductor, short and magnus, soleus gastrognemium, posterior Tibial, Flexor long fingers and hallux, long fibular, short and third (Isometric).

LEVEL AND GOALS:

- Advanced Level;
- Perform movement in the Sagittal plane;
- Mobilize the hip in alternating flexo-extension;
- Perform weight transfer to upper limbs;
- Promote diaphragm strengthening due to pressure of the ball over the abdominal region;
- Promote isometric strengthening of the shoulder girdle and shoulder;
- Promote strengthening of hip extensors and lumbar extensors;
- Promote active stretching of the monoarticular hip flexors and passive stretching of the wrist flexors;
- Favor venous return and lymphatic circulation.

LATERAL FLEXION

Fig. 199

POSITIONS AND ARTICULAR MOVEMENTS

- Cervical, thoracic and lumbar spine: Neutral position in transition for lateral flexion.
- Shoulder: abduction
- Elbow: bilateral flexion
- Hip: neutral in extension.
- Knee: extension
- Ankle: neutral position.

MOVEMENT EXECUTION: in lateral decubitus on the ball the practitioner performs a lateral flexion of the spine contracting the lateral muscles.

ACTIVATED MUSCLES: TRUNK: medial scalene, spine erector, lumbar square, paravertebral, interspinal, oblique (concave column) UPPER LIMBS: Large dorsal.

LEVEL AND GOALS:

- Basic Level;
- Perform movement in the frontal plane;
- Mobilize the spine in lateral flexion;
- Activate and strengthen the lateral musculature of the trunk, anterior and posterior to the side of the concavity;
- Work balance by removing your hand from the ground;
- Promote activation of the trunk muscles for stabilization of the pelvis.

PEACOCK

Fig. 200

POSITIONS AND ARTICULAR MOVEMENTS

- Cervical, thoracic and lumbar spine: from the neutral position in transition to a hyperextension.
- Hip: flexion in transition to extension.
- Knee: extension in transition for gentle flexion

MOVEMENT EXECUTION: in a ventral position on the ball the practitioner performs an extension of the hip and spine, supporting the weight in the ball in the abdominal region, in which the hand support in the ground is almost in the center of the ball.

ACTIVATED MUSCLES: TRUNK: Trapezius upper fibers, spinal erector, lumbar square, paravertebral, oblique, interspinal. UPPER LIMBS: deltoid posterior fibers, large dorsal, rotator cuff, rhomboids, trapezius, triceps, anconeum, LOWER LIMBS: buttocks, ischiatibial, triceps sural.

LEVEL AND GOALS:

- Advanced Level;
- Perform movement in the sagittal plane;
- Mobilize the column in extension;
- Promote active stretching of the anterior neck muscles;
- Activates and strengthens the posterior musculature of the entire spine and lower limbs;
- Work the balance by pulling off the ground and placing your hands in the center of the ball.

KNEE EDUCATION

The exercises illustrated below are made in the primary knee position, in which the starting position will always have as base of support, hands and ball and counted trunk in the ball will be the anterior knife of the legs and sometimes of the thighs. Some of these exercises were extracted from the literature and denominated as conventional while the other exercises are part of the Samiball methodology and were created from the inspiring sources. It is always good to observe and analyze these exercises to be applied correctly, because depending on the patient, student and practitioner, it can be a contraindication, and that each professional in the area identifies it. Most of these exercises present a kinesiological analysis containing information such as: movement execution, positions and joint movements, activated muscles and objectives. Everything for a better comprehension to the reader.

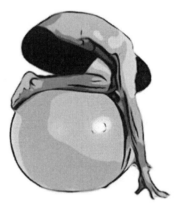

BASIC POINTS

Knee position observations

Ideal Joint Positions:

Fig. 201

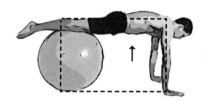
Fig. 202

- Gravity Center is located more in the center, referring to the red line.
- center of the ball.
- Upper limbs supports to help balance.
- It requires greater flexibility of the column extensors, vastus, gluteus maximus, gluteus (posterior portion) and gluteus minimus.
- Perform contraction of the transverse and rectus abdominus, so as not to overload the structures of the lumbar spine (Column Alignment).
- The closer the ball of the feet, the heavier the posture.
- The height of the ball should be the same length as the arm.

Fig. 203

OBS: Before performing the following exercises, it is advised to stretch the wrist extensors because all of these postures are performed with passive wrist extension movement at a 90° angle.

Fig. 204  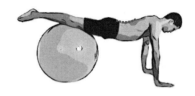 Fig. 205

- GC is placed further forward, referring to the red line.

- Body weight is supported by UPPER LIMBS.

- Without contraction of the transverse and rectus abdominis, it generates an increase in lumbar curvature and an overload in the structures of the lumbar spine. Never stay in this position without the contraction of the abs.

BOUNCER JUMPER

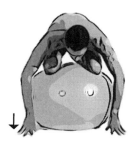
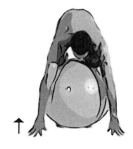

Fig. 206

PARTICULAR MOTIONS AND MOVEMENTS

- Cervical, Thoracic and Lumbar Spine: flexion.
- Scapular girdle: adduction in transition for abduction.
- Shoulder: horizontal abduction in transition for horizontal flexion.
- Elbow: flexion in transition to extension.
- Wrist and fingers: slight extension and extension of fingers.
- Hip: transition flexion for slight extension.
- Knee: flexion.

MOVEMENT EXECUTION: the practitioner performs the movement downward with the trunk and hip pushing the ball down resulting in an abduction of the shoulder accompanied by an elbow flexion.

ACTIVATED MUSCLES: TRUNK: straight abdomen, obliques, UPPER LIMBS: anterior serratus, rhomboid, rotator cuff, trapezius medialis fibers, deltoid, pectoralis major and minor, brachial, biceps brachii, coracobrachial, large dorsal, major and minor round. LOWER LIMBS: iliopsoas, rectus femoris.

LEVEL AND GOALS:

- Moderate level;
- Perform balance movement in the frontal plane;
- Mobilize scapular waist, shoulder and elbow;
- Promote stretching of the posterior muscles of the lumbar spine;
- Activate the muscles of the scapular waist;
- Work on balance and conditioning.

CIRCUNDUCTION

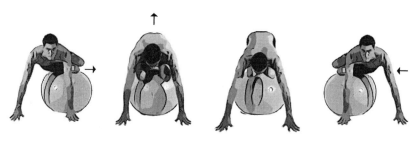

Fig. 207

POSITIONS AND ARTICULAR MOVEMENTS

- Cervical, thoracic and lumbar spine: flexion, rotation and extension.
- Scapular girdle: abduction in transition for adduction and upward rotation.
- Shoulder: horizontal adduction or flexion.
- Wrist and fingers: extension.
- Hip: flexion, slight extension, adduction and abduction.
- Knee: mild flexion in transition for slight extension.

MOVEMENT EXECUTION: knees on the ball, rotates the trunk by pushing the ball to the side, then performs a hip extension by pushing the ball backwards, then flexes with trunk rotation by pushing the ball to the other side and end increases hip flexion by bringing the ball forward. Drawn a circle with the ball.

ACTIVATED MUSCLES: TRUNK: abdomen straight, oblique, transverse abdomen, paravertebral column erector, UPPER LIMBS: rompoid, trapezius medial and inferior fibers, pectoralis major and minor, rotator cuff, major and minor round, deltoid anterior and lateral fibers, triceps, coracobrachial, (biceps brachii, brachial, extensors of the wrist: (isometrically) LOWER LIMBS: iliopsoas, rectus femoris, gluteus medius, minimum, maximum, tensor of fascia lata.

LEVEL AND GOALS:

- Moderate level;
- Perform balance movement in the frontal plane, and transverse;
- Mobilize the spine in rotation, flexion and extension;
- Stretch activate and strengthen the rotator muscles of the spine;
- Mobilize the hip in flexion, extension, abduction and adduction;
- Promote strengthening of the scapular girdle muscles;
- Promote balance and motor coordination.

SNAIL (A) SLIGHT HIP EXTENSION AND FLEXION

Fig. 208

POSITIONS AND ARTICULAR MOVEMENTS

- Cervical column: neutral; Thoracic and Lumbar: transition flexion for a slight extension.
- Shoulder: makes a slight flexion in transition to a slight extension.
- Hip: fulll flexion in transition for a slight extension.
- Knee: full flexion in transition to a slight extension.
- Ankle: neutral in transition to plantar flexion.

MOVEMENT EXECUTION: perform a slight extension of the hip and knee, pushing the ball backwards, returning to the starting position

ACTIVATED MUSCLES: TRUNK: abdominal straight, oblique, paravertebral. UPPER LIMBS: Trapezium, anterior serratil, rotator cuff, coracobrachial, anterior portion deltoid. LOWER LIMBS: iliopsoa, rectus femoris, pectinium, hamstrings, gluteus medialis anterior, gluteus maximus, soleus, gastrognemius and plantar.

LEVEL AND GOALS:

- Moderate level;
- Performing sagging in the sagittal plane;
- Mobilize the hip and knee joints in flexion and extension of approximately 90 degrees;
- Activate hip and knee MUSCLE muscles that are reusable by flexion extension;
- Strengthen two muscles of the shoulder girdle;
- Strengthening of spine stabilizing muscle;
- Work balance;
- Exercises performed in closed kinetic chain for upper limbs;
- Perform passive stretching of the wrist flexors.

SNAIL (B) WITH A COMPLETE HIP AND KNEE EXTENSION AND FLEXION

Fig. 209

POSITIONS AND ARTICULAR MOVEMENTS

- Cervical, thoracic and lumbar spine: transition flexion for full extension.
- Shoulder: 90° bending.
- Elbow: extension.
- Wrist and fingers: extension.
- Hip: full flexion in transition to full extension.
- Knee: full flexion in transition to full extension.
- Ankle: plantar flexion.

MOVEMENT EXECUTION: the practitioner performs the full extension movement of the hip and knee, rolling the ball back, returning to the starting position

ACTIVATED MUSCLES: TRUNK: Abdominal straight, oblique, paravertebral. UPPER LIMBS: Trapezoid, anterior serratil, Manquito rotators, large dorsal, coracobrachial, deltoid anterior portion, triceps, anecdotal. LOWER LIMBS: iliopsoa, rectus femoris, pectinium, hamstrings, gluteus medius anterior portion, gluteus maximus.

LEVEL AND GOALS:

- Performing sagging in the sagittal plane;
- Movement with basic level;
- Mobilize the hip and knee joints in flexion and full extension;
- Activates the muscles responsible for the extension and flexion of the hip and knee;
- Strengthening isometrically the shoulder girdle muscles;
- Strengthening of the abdomen and hip flexors;
- Work balance, generating stability of the trunk;
- Upper limbs closed kinetic chain exercise;
- Perform passive stretching of the wrist flexors.

SCAPULAR PROTRACTION AND RETRACTION

Fig. 210

Fig. 211

POSITIONS AND ARTICULAR MOVEMENTS

- Cervical, thoracic and lumbar spine: neutral.
- Scapular girdle: abduction in transition for adduction.
- Shoulder: flexion.
- Elbow: flexion (fig.211); extension (Fig.210).
- Wrist and fingers: neutral position and Flexion (fig 1 and 2); Extension (fig 3 and 4).
- Hip: extension.
- Knee: extension.
- Ankle: flexing plantar.

MOVEMENT EXECUTION: With the anterior aspect of the thigh on the ball, and support with the forearm (greater base of support) or with the hands (smaller base of support) in the ground, the practitioner realizes a movement of protraction and scapular retraction.

ACTIVATED MUSCLES: TRUNK: paravertebral, rectum of the abdomen, oblique, transverse abdomen, erect spine, lumbar square. UPPER LIMBS: Trapezoid, rhomboid, pectoralis major, serratus anterior, rotator cuff, deltoid anterior fibers, triceps, anechoic (isotonic), biceps brachii, brachial. LOWER LIMBS: gluteus maximus, medius, quadriceps, gastrocnemius, soleus, adductors (isometric).

LEVEL AND GOALS:

- Basic level;
- Perform movement in the sagittal plane;
- Basic movement;
- Promote strengthening of the shoulder flexors (isometrium);
- Strengthen the musculature of the spine (isometry);
- Strengthen the musculature of the shoulder girdle in isotonic form;
- Promotes passive stretching of the wrist flexors.

ABDOMINAL WITH FOREARM ON THE GROUND

Fig. 212

POSITIONS AND ARTICULAR MOVEMENTS

- Cervical spine; thoracic; lumbar: neutral extension in transition to a slight of the lower trunk.

- Scapular girdle: abduction in transition for upward rotation.

- Shoulder: 90° flexion in transition for flexion and approximately 180° degrees.

- Hip: Transition extension for 90° flexion.

- Knee: extension.

- Ankle: neutral.

MOVEMENT EXECUTION: in ventral decertation as the ankle brace supporting the ground, perform the hip flexion movement with a slight flexion of the spine by pulling the ball in the direction of the hand.

ACTIVATED MUSCLES: TRUNK: paravertebral, rectum of the abdomen, oblique, transverse abdomen, erect spine, lumbar square. UPPER LIMBS: Rhomboids, large dorsal, anterior and middle fibers deltoid, biceps, biceps brachii, coracobaquial, pectoralis major, anterior serratil; LOWER LIMBS: Iliopsoas, pectinous, adductor short, long, magno and gracile, vastus, rectus femoral proximal portion, soleus, gastrognêmios.

LEVEL AND GOALS:

- Advanced level;
- Perform the movement in the sagittal plane;
- Work balance;
- Mobilize the hip and shoulder joints in flexion-extension;
- Mobilize the scapular girdle in up and down rotation accompanied by abduction;
- Promote strengthening of the shoulder girdle and the shoulder and elbow;
- Promotes activation and strengthening of the abdominal and posterior muscles of the spine.

PLANK WITH LOWER LIMBS MOVEMENT

Fig. 213

POSITIONS AND ARTICULAR MOVEMENTS

- Cervical, thoracic and lumbar spine: neutral.
- Scapular girdle: abducted and stabilized.
- Shoulder: 90° bending.
- Elbow: extension.
- Fist and fingers: extension.
- Hip: moves from the neutral position in transition to extension, abduction, and flexion of what is in motion.
- Knee: extension of one and the other extension in transition to flexion.
- Ankle: plantar flexion.

MOVEMENT EXECUTION: the practitioner performs an extension, abduction and flexion of the right hip, then returns the limb supported on the ball and performing with the other lower limb.

ACTIVATED MUSCLES: TRUNK: Anterior abdominal muscles lateral and posterior (isometric); UPPER LIMBS: anterior serratus, rotator cuff, trapezius, triceps, large dorsal, anterior deltoid, major and minor pectoral, coracobrachial, triceps, anechoic, brachial (isometrically) LOWER LIMBS: gluteus maximus, ischiostibial proximal portion, gluteus medius and minimal, iliopsoas, rectus femoris, popliteus, leg abductors in motion (isotonic).

LEVEL AND GOALS:

- Moderate level;
- Movement performed in the frontal and sagittal plane;
- Strengthening of the musculature of the shoulder girdle and trunk (isometry);
- Develop balance by removing one of the lower limbs;
- Mobilizes the hip joint in extension, abduction and flexion;
- Activate and strengthen hip muscle and movement;
- Mobilize the knee joint in flexion and extension;
- Promote stretching of the wrist extensor muscles;
- Work Balance;
- Working shoulder and leg proprioception on the ball.

UNIPODAL BALANCE WITH TRUNK ROTATION

Fig. 214

POSITIONS AND ARTICULAR MOVEMENTS

- Cervical spine; Thoracic and Lumbar: neutral extension in transition for right rotation.

- Scapular girdle: abduction in transition for adduction.

- Shoulder: 90° transitional flexion for horizontal abduction.

- Elbow: Extension.

- Fist and fingers: extension in transition to neutral position of the right wrist.

- Hip: extension in transition for flexion of the right.

- Knee: extension in transition for flexion of the right.

- Ankle: plantar flexion in transition to neutral right positio.

MOVEMENT EXECUTION: the practitioner in the supine position, with his / her hands resting on the ground, with his / her legs on the ball, performs a hip flexion and right knee disengaging of the ball. Then it takes the right foot between the two hands, after supporting the foot to withdraw the hand right of the ground and takes up making a rotation to the right of the whole column. Staying for a few seconds and doing to the other side.

ACTIVATED MUSCLES: TRUNK: Ecoms, scalenes, Oblique, rotators, multifidus, rectus abdominis, transverse abdomen, spinal erectors. UPPER LIMBS: rhomboids, anterior serratil, trapezius medial and inferior fibers, pectoralis major (of the limb supported on the ground), large and minor round, deltoid fibers anterior and lateral and posterior of the raised arm, coracobrachial, triceps, anechoic, supraspinal e biceps. LOWER LIMBS: iliopsoas adductor long, short and magnu, gracilis, hamstrings and extensions, gluteus maximus and mid anterior fibers of the right leg, gluteus medius posterior fibers, gluteus maximus, minimum, maximum, vast and rectus femoris left leg.

LEVEL AND GOALS:

- •Advanced level;
- Perform movement in the oblique plane;
- Work balance;
- Movement with a high level of execution;
- Mobilize the spine in rotation, lengthening and activating rotator muscles;
- Mobilize the hip in flexion, extension of the right and extension of the left hip flexors;
- Promote strengthening of the scapular girdle muscles;
- Promote activation and strengthening of right thigh muscle.

PARTIAL AND COMPLETE TRUNK ROTATION

Fig. 215   Fig. 216

POSITIONS AND ARTICULAR MOVEMENTS

- Neutral cervical column; Thoracic and Lumbar: rotation from one side to another.
- Shoulder: horizontal adduction.
- Elbow extension.
- Fist and fingers: extension.
- Hip: flexion.
- Knee: flexion.
- Ankle: plantar flexion.

MOVEMENT EXECUTION: the practitioner performs a slight rotation of the spine to one side and the other, rolling the ball to one side and the other.

ACTIVATED MUSCLES: TRUNK: abdomen straight, oblique, transverse abdomen, paravertebral column erector. UPPER LIMBS: rhomboids, trapezius medial and inferior fibers, pectoralis major and minor, major and minor round, deltoid anterior and lateral fibers, triceps, coracobrachial, (brachial biceps, brachial, wrist extensors: isometrically) LOWER LIMBS: iliopsoas, rectus femoris, gluteus maximus, minimum, maximum, tensor of fascia lata.

LEVEL AND GOALS:

- Moderate level;
- Perform balance movement in the frontal plane, and transverse;
- Movement with the moderate level;
- Mobilize the lower trunk in rotation, lengthening and activating the muscles responsible for rotation;
- Work proprioception of upper limbs joint;
- Promote strengthening of the scapular girdle muscles;
- Promote activation and strengthening of the spinal muscles.

TRUNK ROTATION WITH LOWER LIMB ABDUCTION

Fig. 217

POSITIONS AND ARTICULAR MOVEMENTS

- Cervical column: neutral or extension; Thoracic and Lumbar: rotation from one side to another.
- Shoulder: 90° Flexion.
- Elbow: extension.
- Fist and fingers: extension.
- Hip: flexion with abduction movement of the leg above.
- Knee: flexion in transition to extension of the leg above.
- Ankle: plantar flexion.

MOVEMENT EXECUTION: the practitioner rotates the spine to one side, abducting the lower limb above, rolling the ball to the other side and doing the abduction of the other leg.

ACTIVATED MUSCLES: TRUNK: abdomen straight, oblique, transverse abdomen, paravertebral column erector. UPPER LIMBS: rhomboids, trapezius medial and inferior fibers, pectoralis major and minor, major and minor round, deltoid anterior and lateral fibers, triceps, coracobrachial , (brachii, brachial, wrist extensors: isometrically) LOWER LIMBS: iliopsoas, rectus femoris, gluteus maximus, minimum, maximum, tensor of fascia lata, soleus, gastrognemium of limb to be above.

LEVEL AND GOALS:

- Moderate level;
- Perform balance movement in the frontal plane, and transverse.
- Mobilizes the lower spine in rotation, lengthening the rotator muscles contralateral to the movement.
- Mobilizes the hip in abduction and adduction.
- Promotes strengthening of the abductors of the limb above.
- Promote isometric strengthening of the scapular girdle muscles.
- Promote balance.

ÊKAPADA KÁKASÁNA-ARABESQUE

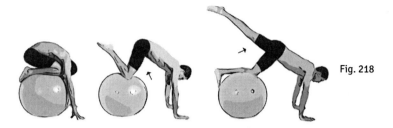

Fig. 218

POSITIONS AND ARTICULAR MOVEMENTS

- Cervical, thoracic and lumbar spine: slight transitional flexion for slight extension.
- Shoulder: bilateral flexion.
- Elbow: bilateral extension.
- Fist and fingers: bilateral extension.
- Hip: transition flexion for elevated limb extension
- Knee: flexion in transition for extension of the raised limb.
- Ankle: plantar flexion in transition for dorsiflexion of the foot supported on the ball.

MOVEMENT EXECUTION: the practitioner with the knees on the ball performs an extension of the hip and knee of one of the limbs raising the foot.

ACTIVATED MUSCLES: TRUNK: abdomen straight, oblique, transverse abdomen, paravertebral column erector. UPPER LIMBS: anterior serratil, rotator cuff, trapezius, pectoralis major, coracobrachial deltoid, biceps long portion, triceps, anecdotal; aneurysm. LOWER LIMBS: gluteus maximus, gluteus medius posterior portion, hamstrings of the raised leg.

LEVEL AND GOALS:

- Advanced Level;
- Perform movement in the frontal plane;
- Mobilize the hip and knee flexion-extension;
- Promote strengthening of the hip extensors of the leg above;
- Promote strengthening of the scapular (isometric) waist and trunk muscles;
- Work balance

TRUNK ROTATION WITH ELBOW FLEXION AND LOWER LIMB EXTENSION

Fig. 219

POSITIONS AND ARTICULAR MOVEMENT

- Cervical spine; Neutral; Thoracic and Lumbar: flexion in transition for rotation.

- Shoulder: transition flexion for horizontal abduction

- Elbow: extension in transition for flexion.

- Fist and fingers: extension.

- Hip: transition flexion for alternate extension of the limb above.

- Knee: flexion in transition for extension of one of the knees.

- Ankle: neutral position in transition for plantar flexion.

MOVEMENT EXECUTION: the practitioner with the legs on the ball and hands on the ground, rotates the spine to one side, extending the lower limb on top, then makes an elbow flexion approaching the thorax of the ground, make the movements to the other side.

ACTIVATED MUSCLES: TRUNK: abdomen straight, oblique, transverse abdomen, paravertebral column erector, UPPER LIMBS: anterior serrtistil, rotator cuff, rhomboids, trapezius medial and inferior fibers, pectoralis major and minor, round larger and smaller, deltoid fibers anterior and lateral, triceps, coracobrachial, (biceps brachii, brachial, extensors of wrist (isometric) LOWER LIMBS: gluteus, quadriceps, triceps sural.

LEVEL AND GOALS:

- Advanced level;
- Perform movement in the frontal plane, and transverse;
- Mobilize the spine in rotation;
- Work balance and stimulate proprioception;
- Mobilize the hip in flexo-extension;
- Promote strengthening of abductors and extensors of the lower limb above;
- Promote strengthening of the shoulder girdle, flexor and shoulder adductor muscles;
- Promote strengthening of the elbow flexors and extensors;
- Promote passive stretching by the ball of hip abductors flexed on the ball.

PLANK WITH TRUNK ROTATION AND EXTENDED LOWER LIMBS

Fig. 220

POSITIONS AND ARTICULAR MOVEMENTS

- Cervical, thoracic and lumbar spine: neutral extension in transition for rotation.
- Shoulder: 90º bending or horizontal adduction.
- Elbow: extension.
- Fist and fingers: extension.
- Hip: extension.
- Knee: extension.
- Ankle: plantar flexion.

MOVEMENT EXECUTION: the practitioner rotates the spine to one side and the other by rolling the ball back and forth with the lower limb extended.

ACTIVATED MUSCLES: TRUNK: Oblique, rectum of the abdomen, transverse of the abdomen, erector of the spine, paravertebral, transespinhais UPPER LIMBS: rotator cuff, anterior serratil, rhomboids, trapezius medial and inferior fibers, pectoralis major and minor, round bigger and smaller, deltoid fibers anterior and lateral, triceps, coracobrachial, (biceps brachii, brachialis, wrist extensors: isometrically.

LEVEL AND GOALS:

- Advanced level;
- Perform movement in the transverse plane;
- Mobilizes the spine in rotation;
- Promote activation and strengthening of rotator muscles;
- Promotes isometric strengthening of the scapular girdle and elbow extensor muscles;
- Work balance;
- Promotes passive stretching of the wrist flexors.

(RÁJA KAKÁSANA) SHOULDER FLEXION AND EXTENSION

Fig. 221

POSITIONS AND ARTICULAR MOVEMENTS

- Cervical, Thoracic and Lumbar Spine: flexion.
- Shoulder: lightly bending in transition to slight extension
- Elbow: extension.
- Fist and fingers: slight flexion in transition to slight extension.
- Hip: transition flexion for slight extension.
- Knee: flexion in transition to slight extension.
- Ankle: dorsal flexion.

MOVEMENT EXECUTION: the practitioner performs a slight extension and flexion of the shoulder, pushing the ball back and forth.

ACTIVATED MUSCLES: TRUNK: Straight abdominal, oblique, transverse abdomen, erector spindles (eccentric) UPPER LIMBS: rotator cuff, anterior serratil, rompoid, trapezius medial and inferior fibers, pectoralis major and minor, major and minor round, deltoid anterior fibers and lateral, triceps, coracobrachial, (biceps brachii, brachial, extensors of the wrist: isometrically LOWER LIMBS: iliopsoas, ischium, quadriceps (eccentric) anterior tibial.

LEVEL AND GOALS:

- Advanced level;
- Performing sagging in the sagittal plane;
- Promote strengthening of the muscles in the shoulder girdle and the shoulders and elbows;
- Promote flexo-extension shoulder mobilization;
- Promote wrist mobilization in flexo-extension and passive stretching of the flexors of the wrist;
- Promote strengthening of the abs;
- Increase the direction of blood flow to the head area.

PLANK WITH LOWER TRUNK LATERAL FLEXION (LUMBAR SPINE)

Fig. 222

POSITIONS AND ARTICULAR MOVEMENTS

- Cervical column: neutral; Thoracic and Lumbar: Alternate lateral flexion, with a slight rotation of the inferior trunk.
- Shoulder: flexion.
- Elbow: extension.
- Fist and fingers: extension.
- Hip: alternate adduction and abduction of limbs.
- Knee: extension.
- Ankle: plantar flexion.

MOVEMENT EXECUTION: the practitioner performs a slight lateral flexion of the lumbar spine, pushing the ball to one side and the other, passively alternating adduction and abduction of the leg due to the movement of the lateral slope of the spine.

ACTIVATED MUSCLES: TRUNK: Internal and external oblique, lumbar square, spine erector, paravertebral, unilateral abdominal rectus. UPPER LIMBS: rotator cuff, anterior serratus, rhomboids, mid and upper trapezius, major and minor pectoralis, anterior portion deltoid, coracobrachial, triceps, anecdotal. LOWER LIMBS: wrist extensors: mid and gluteus maximus, fascia lata tensor, long and short.

LEVEL AND GOALS:

- Moderate level;
- Perform balance movement in the frontal plane;
- Strengthening the shoulder girdle (isometric) and shoulders;
- Mobilize the lower spine in lateral flexion;
- Strengthening of the muscle muscles responsible for lateral flexion (isotonic);
- Passive stretching of wrist extensors.

PLANK WITH ELBOW FLEXION AND EXTENSION

Fig. 223

POSITIONS AND ARTICULAR MOVEMENTS

- Cervical, thoracic and lumbar spine: neutral extension.
- Shoulder girdle: neutral in transition to adduction.
- Shoulder: transition flexion for horizontal abduction.
- Elbow: extension in transition for flexion.
- Fist and fingers: extension.
- Hip: neutral extension.
- Knee: extension.
- Ankle: plantar flexion.

MOVEMENT EXECUTION: the practitioner does the elbow flexion accompanied by an abduction of the shoulder bringing the chest close to the ground.

ACTIVATED MUSCLES: TRUNK: trapezius upper fibers, Oblique, rectus abdominis, transverse abdomen, paravertebral, erectile spine. UPPER LIMBS: Rotator cuff, anterior serratil, rhomboids, trapezius, pectoralis major and minor, coracobrachial, triceps, anconeous, large round, large dorsal. LOWER LIMBS: hamstrings, adductor magnus, gluteus maximus (concentric), ilipsoas, rectus femoris (Eccentric), for the neutral extension of the hips, vast for the neutral extension of the knee, soleus, posterior tibial, fibular third, short and long flexor long fingers and the hallux and gastrognemium for plantar flexion.

LEVEL AND GOALS:

- Moderate level;
- Perform movement in the frontal and sagittal plane;
- Movement from basic to moderate level;
- Movement realized in closed kinetic chain of the upper limbs;
- Strengthening of the spinal muscles, especially the cervical spine (isometric);
- Strengthening of the musculature of the shoulder girdle responsible for adduction and scapular abduction (isotonic);
- Strengthening shoulder muscles responsible for adduction and horizontal abduction. (isotonic);
- Strengthening of the musculature responsible for elbow flexion and extension (isotonic);
- Passive elongation of the wrist flexors.

OBS.: Be careful not to move the shoulder of the elbow line and increase the external rotation of the shoulder, and to overload the ligaments.

PLANK WITH SHOULDER FLEXION AND EXTENSION

Fig. 224

POSITIONS AND ARTICULAR MOVEMENTS

- Cervical column: neutral extension; Thoracic and Lumbar: neutral extension in transition for mild hyper-extension.
- Scapular girdle: neutral in transition for upward rotation.
- Shoulder: 90° flexion in transition for 180° bending.
- Elbow: extension.
- Fist and fingers: extension.
- Hip: extension.
- Knee: extension.
- Ankle: plantar flexion.

MOVEMENT EXECUTION: the practitioner flexes the shoulder and the trunk moves backward by rolling the ball in the same direction, performing a spinal hyperextension.

ACTIVATED MUSCLES: TRUNK: trapezius upper fibers, oblique, rectus abdominis, transverse abdomen, paravertebral, erectile spine. LOWER LIMBS: hamstrings, adductor magnus, gluteus maximus (concentric), ilipsoas, rectus femoris (Eccentric), to the neutral extension. of the hips, vast for the neutral extension of the knee, soleus, posterior tibial, third fibular, short and long, flexor long fingers and hallux and gastrognemium for plantar flexion.

LEVEL AND GOALS:

- Moderate level;
- Perform balance sheet movement;
- Movement realized in closed kinetic chain of the upper limbs;
- Strengthen the spinal muscles, especially the cervical spine. (isometric);
- Strengthen the musculature of the shoulder girdle responsible for upward rotation (isotonic);
- Activate and strengthen the shoulder muscles responsible for horizontal flexion and extension. (Isotonic);
- Passive elongation of wrist flexors.

(VRISHKÁSANA) HIP FLEXION AND EXYENSION

Fig. 225

POSITIONS AND ARTICULAR MOVEMENTS

- Thoracic and Lumbar Spine: neutral in extension in transition to hyperextension.
- Shoulder girdle: neutral position.
- Shoulder: bend approximately 90º.
- Hip: flexion in transition to extension.
- Knee: extension.
- Ankle: dorsal flexion in transition to plantar flexion

MOVEMENT EXECUTION: the practitioner performs an extension of the lower trunk and the hip, raising the feet.

WORKING MUSCLES: TRUNK: Erectors of the spine lumbar region, lumbar square, paravertebral, oblique. UPPER LIMBS: Anterior serratil, rhomboids, pectoralis major, deltoid anterior fibers, triceps, anchovy, coracobrachial, biceps braquail, brachial. LOWER LIMBS: gluteus maximus, biceps femoris, semitendinosus, semimembranosus, gluteus medius posterior portion, adutor magno.

LEVEL AND GOALS:

- Moderate level;
- Perform movement in the sagittal plane;
- Movement with the moderate level;
- Mobilize the lumbar spine in flexion and extension;
- Mobilize the hip in flexo-extension;
- Strengthen the posterior spinal muscles (spine erector, lumbar square), paravertebral and hip extensors (gluteus maximus, medial posterior fibers, proximal portion hamstrings);
- Promote scapular stability and strengthen scapular girdle muscles (isometrically); anterior serratil, rhomboid, pectoral and deltoid closed-chain muscles;
- Promote balance;
- Promote strengthening of the diaphragm, generated by the pressure of the ball in the abdominal region pushing the viscera;
- Due to the severity of the blood flow to the head region.

PLANK WITH HIP RAISING

Fig. 226

POSITIONS AND ARTICULAR MOVEMENTS

- Cervical, thoracic and lumbar spine: from the neutral extension in transition to slight flexion of the inferior trunk
- Shoulder girdle: neutral position in transition for upward rotation.
- Shoulder: 90° flexion in transition to 180° flexion.
- Elbow: extension.
- Fist and fingers: extension.
- Hip: extension.
- Knee: extension.
- Ankle: plantar flexion.

MOVEMENT EXECUTION: the practitioner flexes the hip and lower torso by pulling the ball toward the arms.

WORKING MUSCLES: TRUNK: Intertransversal muscles, transverse abdomen, rectus abdominis, oblique, erector spine to stabilize spine, upper trapezius. UPPER LIMBS: anterior Serratil, rhomboids, trapezius middle and lower portion, deltoid anterior portion, coracobrachial, biceps long portion, triceps, anus, flexors of the wrist. LOWER LIMBS: Ilipsoas, pectinio, adductor magno and long and short to maintain the hip in adduction.

LEVEL AND GOALS:

- Moderate to advanced level;
- Perform movement in the sagittal plane of the shoulder, hip and lower trunk;
- Move in closed kinetic chain of the upper limbs;
- Strengthen the muscles responsible for flexion and extension of the hip and shoulder (isotonic);
- Strengthen the spine flexors;
- Passive elongation of the wrist flexors;
- Work balance and strength;
- Movement with an intermediate degree of difficulty.

PLANK WITH HIP RAISING AND FLEXED SHOULDER AT 180 DEGREES

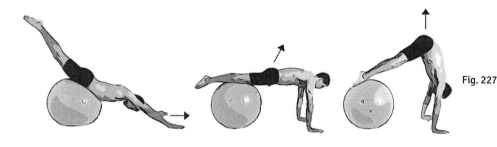

Fig. 227

POSITIONS AND ARTICULAR MOVEMENTS

- Cervical, thoracic and lumbar spine: transitional neutral extension for slight flexion of the lower trunk
- Shoulder girdle: rotation up.
- Shoulder: 180° bending.
- Elbow: extension.
- Fist and fingers: extension.
- Hip: extension in transition for 90° flexion.
- Knee: extension.
- Ankle: plantar flexion.

MOVEMENT EXECUTION: the practitioner flexes the shoulder and the trunk moves backward by rolling the ball in the same direction and then flexing the shoulder and hip by pulling the ball forward with the lower limb extended, touching the dorsum of the foot on the ball, returning to the starting position.

WORKING MUSCLES: TRUNK: Intertransversal muscles, transverse abdomen, rectus abdominis, oblique, erector spine to stabilize spine, upper trapezius. UPPER LIMBS: Trapezius, anterior serratil, rhomboids, deltoid, coracobrabruial, triceps, anchovy, biceps brachii, flexors. of the wrist (eccentrically) LOWER LIMBS: gluteus maximus, gluteus medius posterior and anterior portion, hamstrings.

LEVEL AND GOALS:

- Moderate to advanced level;
- Performing sagging in the sagittal plane;
- Perform movement in the sagittal plane;
- Strengthen the abdominal muscles, shoulder girdle and flexors and extensors of the hip. (isotonic);
- Promote active flexor extension of the wrist;
- Movement with a high degree of difficulty;
- Promote proprioceptive stimulation of the shoulders and elbow.

SCORPION (HORIZONTAL ABDUCTION TO SHOULDER FLEXION)

Fig. 228

POSITIONS AND ARTICULAR MOVEMENTS

- Cervical, thoracic and lumbar spine: transitional neutral extension for mild thoracic and lumbar hyperextension.
- Shoulder girdle: adduction in transition for upward rotation.
- Shoulder: horizontal abduction in transition for flexion.
- Elbow: flexion in transition to extension.
- Handle and fingers: extension in transition to neutral position.
- Hip: extension.
- Knee: extension.
- Ankle: plantar flexion.

MOVEMENT EXECUTION: the practitioner with horizontal abduction shoulders and flexed elbows extends the elbow with a shoulder flexion, pushing the ball backward, projecting the chest back and forth always close to the ground by pushing the ball forward and back.

ACTIVATED MUSCLES: TRUNK: intertransversal muscles, transverse abdomen, rectus abdominis, oblique, erector spine to stabilize spine, upper trapezius. UPPER LIMBS: serrátil anterior, trapezium, pectoralis major, deltoite fibers middle and anterior. LOWER LIMBS: gluteus maximus, gluteus posterior portion, ischiatibialis and adductors to keep the hip in extension and adducted.

LEVEL AND GOALS:

- Moderate level;
- Movement performed in the oblique plane;
- Promote strengthening of the shoulder girdle and shoulder flexor muscles;
- Promote active stretching of the shoulder extensor;
- Promote activation of the lateral muscles of the lumbar spine to maintain stability of the ball;
- Promote proprioceptive stimulation of the shoulders and elbows;
- Promote passive stretching of the wrist flexors;

OBS: Take care of the shoulder in passing the elbow line thus increasing the external rotation.

DEVELOPMENT (ELBOW FLEXION AND EXTENSION WITH A RAISED HIP)

Fig. 229

POSITIONS AND ARTICULAR MOVEMENTS

- Cervical, thoracic and lumbar spine: slight flexion
- Shoulder girdle: rotation up in transition for downward rotation.
- Shoulder: transition flexion for horizontal abduction.
- Elbow: extension in transition for flexion.
- Fist and fingers: extension.
- Hip: flexion.
- Knee: extension.
- Ankle: plantar flexion.

MOVEMENT EXECUTION: the practitioner with the back of the feet supported on the ball and with the gluteus elevated, performs a flexion and extension of the elbow approaching and distancing the forehead of the ground.

ACTIVATED MUSCLES: TRUNK: Strain of the abdomen, Transespinalis, oblique and erector of the spine with stabilizers. UPPER LIMBS: Anterior serratil, trapezius, pectoralis minor, scapula elevator, deltoid, supraspinatus, coracobrachial. LOWER LIMBS: Iliopsoas, rectus femoris, vastus , soleus, short and long fibular.

LEVEL AND GOALS:

- Advanced Level;
- Movement performed in oblique plane;
- Promote mobilization of the joints of the shoulder girdle, shoulder and elbow;
- Promote strengthening of the shoulder girdle muscles, which are responsible for upward rotation and downward and shoulder rotation;
- Promote isometric strengthening of the spinal and hip flexors;
- Promote passive stretching of the wrist flexors;
- Promote proprioceptive stimulation of shoulder and elbow articulations.

KNEE ON THE BALL

Fig. 230

MOVEMENT EXECUTION: Remove the heels from the ground, both feet, leaving only the tip of the metatarsals, then transfer the weight of the body forward, remove one foot and then remove the other, placing the knees in the ball with the hands (4 supports), balancing in this position, withdraw one hand (3 supports) and then the other hand, with the knees in the ball and the hip flexed to dominate the balance. By mastering this position the person makes a hip stretch getting into a more upright posture.

LEVEL AND GOALS:

- Movement with moderate to advanced level;
- Promote balance;
- Work the postural reactions (balance, rectification and straightening;
- Promote activation of the abdominal muscles by keeping the ball stabilized;
- Develop concentration;
- Develop self-confidence in the ball.

OBS: Avoid in people who have some type of dizziness;.

ONE FOOT STANCE WITH KNEE

Fig. 231

POSITIONS AND ARTICULAR MOVEMENTS

- Cervical, thoracic and lumbar spine: neutral extension.

- Shoulder: transition neutral extension for abduction.

- Elbow: slight flexion in transition for light supination accompanied by slight flexion.

- Wrist and fingers: light extension in transition to neutral extension.

- Hip: bilateral flexion but the right with greater amplitude and the lower left

- Knee: bilateral flexion.

- Ankle: left and right flexor plantar flexion.

MOVEMENT EXECUTION: with the right foot and front face of the left leg on the ball and with the hands on the ball, the practitioner removes his hands from the ball making a slight extension of the spine trying to be as aligned as possible.

ACTIVATED MUSCLES: TRUNK: Straight abdomen, oblique, paravertebral, erector spine, lumbar square. UPPER LIMBS: Manquito rotators, deltoid lateral and posterior fibers, rhomboids, trapezium fibers medium. LOWER LIMBS: Iliopsoas, ischium, adductor, tibialis anterior (foot resting on the ball).

LEVEL AND GOALS:

- Moderate to advanced level;
- Promote balance;
- Exercise with a high standard of difficulty;
- Work on postural reactions (balance, rectification and straightening;
- Promote activation of the abdominal muscles by keeping the ball stabilized;
- Develop concentration;
- Develop self-confidence on the ball.

OBS: Avoid in people who have some type of dizziness.

SQUATTING ON THE BALL

Fig. 232

POSITIONS AND ARTICULAR MOVEMENTS

- Cervical, thoracic and lumbar spine: slight flexion.
- Shoulder: adduction in transition for abduction.
- Elbow: extension in transition for flexion.
- Handle and fingers: extension in transition to neutral position.
- Hip: full bilateral flexion.
- Knee: full bilateral flexion.
- Ankle: plantar flexion accompanied by inversion.

MOVEMENT EXECUTION: with his feet and hands resting on the ball, the practitioner withdraws one hand and then withdraws the other hand, leaving only with his feet on the ball in the crouching position.

ACTIVATED MUSCLES: TRUNK: Straight abdomen, oblique, paravertebral, erector spine, lumbar square. UPPER LIMBS: Rotator Cuff, deltoid lateral and posterior fibers, Romboids, trapezium medium fibers, wrist extensors. LOWER LIMBS: Iliopsoas, ischium, adductor, inverter, anterior tibial.

LEVEL AND GOALS:

- Advanced level;
- Promote balance;
- Exercise with a high standard of difficulty;
- Work the postural reactions (balance, rectification and straightening;
- Promote activation of the scapular girdle muscles;
- Promote activation of abdominal and MMMII muscles by keeping the ball stabilized;
- Develop concentration;
- Develop self-confidence in the ball.

OBS: Avoid this exercise in people who get dizzy.

ORTHOSTATIC POSITION ON THE BALL

Fig. 233

POSITIONS AND ARTICULAR MOVEMENTS

- Cervical, thoracic and lumbar spine: flexion in transition for neutral extension.
- Shoulder girdle: abduction in transition to neutral position.
- Shoulder: flexion in transition to neutral extension.
- Elbow: extension.
- Wrist and fingers: extension for neutral transition.
- Hip: flexion in transition to extension.
- Knee: flexion in transition to extension.
- Ankle: slight plantar flexion accompanied by eversion.

MOVEMENT EXECUTION: crouching with four supports on the ball, the person after finding the balance performs an extension of the spine, hip and knee, lifting the body, standing on the ball.

ACTIVATED MUSCLES: TRUNK: Spine, interspinal, semi-spinal erector spines of the neck and thorax to keep the spine in neutral extension. LOWER LIMBS: Max buttocks, medium posterior and medium portion, long, short and magnu adductors, femoral straight, vast, gastrognemius.

LEVEL AND GOALS:

- Advanced level;
- Work the postural reactions (balance, rectification and straightening;
- Promote activation of the abdominal muscles by keeping the ball stabilized;
- Develops concentration;
- Promote strengthening of the adductors, hip extensors, and knee extensors and flexors;
- Develop self-confidence on the ball.

PENDULUM

Fig. 234

MOVEMENT EXECUTION: with the body, the person will roll from the knees, hips, abdomen and chest to the chest area, placing their hands on the ground stopping the movement and supporting the body on the ball.

ACTIVATED MUSCLES: complex movement, to facilitate only the last posture: posterior muscles of the body will be analyzed.

LEVEL AND GOALS:

- Advanced level;
- Work the postural reactions (balance, rectification and straightening;

- Promote activation and strengthening of the extensor muscles of the spine, hip;
- Develop concentration;
- Promote activation and strengthening of the scapular girdle muscles;
- Develop self-confidence on the ball.

WALL EDUCATION

The movements shown below were created to be performed with the using the parade. It is a challenging and challenging work, in which the starting position will always be based on the ball and on the wall, hands and / or feet. The counted body on the ball will be the torso or the ischia. These exercises, due to their positioning will always require great activations of the spinal flexors. It is always good to observe and analyze these exercises to be applied correctly, because depending on the patient, student and practitioner it can be a contraindication because it involves a lot of balance and muscular activation of the anterior chain. These exercises present a kinesiological analysis containing information such as the movement execution, positions and joint movements, activated muscles and objectives.

STANDING ON THE SOLE OF FEET

POSITIONS AND ARTICULAR MOVEMENTS

• Cervical, thoracic and lumbar spine: slight flexion.

• Shoulder: flexion in transition to neutral extension.

• Elbow: extension.

• Wrist and fingers: extension in transition to neutral.

• Hip: flexion.

• Knee: flexion.

• Ankle: plantar flexion.

Fig. 235

MOVEMENT EXECUTION: sitting on the ball, the practitioner places both hands on the wall as initial support, beginning to remove the feet from the ground and leading to the wall, one after the other, with the frames on the wall and after the feet, the practitioner removes his hands from the wall and carries out a slight extension of the spine.

ACTIVATED MUSCLES: TRUNK: Anterior straight head, and straight lateral head, long head and neck, bilateral ecomus, abdominal straight, bilateral oblique (stabilizers); UPPER LIMBS: In the support of the hand on the wall (anterior portion deltoid, coracobrachial, anterior serratil, large dorsal and extensors of the wrist); LOWER LIMBS: Rectus femoris, iliopoas, pectineum, adductors, tibialis anterior, fibularis third.

LEVEL AND GOALS:

- Moderate level;
- Movement realized in closed kinetic chain;
- Perform movement in the sagittal plane;
- Promote self-confidence;
- Promote activation of the anterior chain muscles of the spine due to the action of gravity;
- Strengthening (isometric) the spinal flexors;
- Promote activation of the lateral muscles of the trunk, by stabilizing the ball, avoiding that it roll to the sides;
- Promote proprioceptive stimulation in the soles of the feet.

HIP AND KNEE FLEXION-EXTENSION

POSITIONS AND ARTICULAR MOVEMENTS

- Cervical, thoracic and lumbar spine: slight flexion.
- Shoulder: neutral extension.
- Elbow: neutral extension.
- Wrist and fingers: Slight flexion.
- Hip: flexion.
- Knee: flexion in transition to extension.
- Ankle: dorsal flexion in transition to plantar flexion.

Fig. 236

MOVEMENT EXECUTION: Sitting on the ball with feet propped against the wall, the practitioner performs an extension and flexion of the hip and knee pushing the ball back and forth.

ACTIVATED MUSCLES: TRUNK: Anterior straight head, and lateral straight head, long head and neck, bilateral ecom, abdominal straight, bilateral oblique (stabilizers). LOWER LIMBS: Iliopsoas, rectus femoris, pectini, adductors, Gluteus anterior portion, Gluteus minimus, vastus, hamstrings, popliteus, tibialis anterior, fibularis third.

GOAL:

- Basic Level;
- Perform sagittal plane movement;
- Promote self-confidence;
- Mobilize the hip and knee joint in flexo-extension;
- Activate the muscles responsible for the movement of the hip and knee;
- Strengthening (isometric) the spinal flexors;
- Promote proprioceptive stimulation on the soles of the feet;
- Promote activation of the lateral and posterior muscles of the spine, by stabilizing the ball, avoiding that it roll to the sides;
- Promote stretching of the posterior MUSCLE muscles of the lower limbs when the knee is in extension;
- Promote stretching of spine, lumbar and hip extensors when the practitioner has a hip and knee flexed, with the gluteus next to the wall;
- Promote activation of the anterior chain muscles of the spine due to gravity action.

ROTACIONAL

POSITIONS AND ARTICULAR MOVEMENTS

- Cervical, Thoracic and Lumbar Column: flexion with lateral flexion accompanied by rotation.

- Shoulder: horizontal abduction and extension

- Elbow: flexion.

- Wrist and fingers: flexion.

- Hip: flexion with alternating adduction and abduction movement.

Fig. 237

- Knee: extension in transition for flexion, alternating the knees.

- Ankle: plantar flexion in transition to dorsiflexion with alternating inversion.

MOVEMENT EXECUTION: sitting on the ball and feet propped against the wall, the practitioner performs a rotation of the trunk, rolling the ball to the sides, flexing the knee contralateral to rotation.

ACTIVATED MUSCLES: TRUNK: Anterior straight head, lateral straight head, long head and neck, lateral bilateral, abdominal straight, bilateral oblique, spinal erector in unilateral contraction. UPPER LIMBS: deltoid, supraspinatus, small round, biceps long portion. LOWER LIMBS: iliopsoas, pectineum, rectus femoris, ischiatibialis, adductors, long fibular, short and tibialis anterior.

LEVEL AND GOALS:

- Moderate level;
- Movement realized in closed kinetic chain;
- Perform movement in the oblique plane;
- Promote weight transfer sideways;
- Work balance and coordination;
- Promote activation of the spinal flexor and rotator muscles;
- Promote isometric strengthening of the spinal flexors;
- Promote isotonic strengthening of the lateral flexors and rotators of the alternating and unilateral column of the abdominal;
- Promote stretching of the posterior muscles and external rotators of the lower limb that has an outstretched knee;
- Promote hip mobilization in adduction and abduction;
- Promote proprioceptive stimulation of the soles of the feet on the wall;
- Promote activation of the anterior and crossed spinal chain muscles due to the gravity action;
- Work balancing reactions protection and rectification.

HIP AND SPINE FLEXION

POSITIONS AND ARTICULAR MOVEMENTS

Fig. 238

- Cervical Column: Neutral; Thoracic and Lumbar: transition flexion for extension or flexion in transition for rotation.
- Shoulder: bilateral neutral.
- Elbow: bilateral Flexion.
- Wrist and fingers: neutral extension.
- Hip: transition flexion for slight extension.
- Knee: flexion.
- Ankle: dorsal flexion.

MOVEMENT EXECUTION: sitting on the ball with feet propped against the wall, the practitioner performs an extension and flexion of the spine with the hands resting on the chest or behind the head.

ACTIVATED MUSCLES: TRUNK: Forehead straight and lateral straight head, long head and neck, bilateral sternocleidomastoid (isometric) Straight and transverse abdominal, bilateral internal and external oblique (stabilizers), spinal erector. LOWER LIMBS: iliopsoas, rectus femoris (proximal portion).

ABDOMINAL WITH SPINE ROTATION
(variation)

POSITIONS AND ARTICULAR MOVEMENTS

Fig. 239

• Thoracic and Lumbar Spine: extension in transition for flexion accompanied by rotation.

MOVEMENT EXECUTION: sitting on the ball with feet propped against the wall, the practitioner performs an extension and flexion of the spine with his hands resting on his chest.

ACTIVATED MUSCLES: TRUNK: Forehead straight and lateral straight, long head and neck, bilateral (isometric) straight and transverse abdominal, bilateral internal and external oblique (stabilizers), spinal erectors and spinal transverse. LOWER LIMBS: iliopsoas, rectus femoris proximal portion.

LEVEL AND GOALS:

- Moderate level;
- Perform motion in the oblique plane;
- Movement at a moderate level;
- Work balance;
- Promote strengthening of the spinal flexors and rotators;
- Mobilize the spine and flexion-extension with rotation;
- Promote proprioceptive stimulation in the soles of the feet with the wall.

SUPINE ON THE BALL AND FEET ON THE WALL

POSITIONS AND ARTICULAR MOVEMENTS

Fig. 240

- Cervical, thoracic and lumbar spine: transition flexion for neutral extension

- Shoulder: flexion in transition to neutral extension.

- Elbow: slight flexion in transition to extension.

- Handle and fingers: extension in transition to neutral position.

- Hip: transition flexion for extension.

- Knee: flexion in transition to extension.

- Ankle: dorsal flexion in transition to neutral position.

MOVEMENT EXECUTION: sitting on the ball with his feet and hands resting on the wall, the practitioner will remove his hands from the wall, performing an extension of the hips and knees, rolling the ball back a little, stopping the movement when it is with the whole body lying in the ventral decubitus.

ACTIVATED MUSCLES: TRUNK: Forehead straight and lateral straight head, long head and neck, bilateral (isometric) straight and transverse abdominal, bilateral internal and external oblique (stabilizers), spine erectors, Transespinalis. UPPER LIMBS: Deltoid, coracobrachial, pectoralis major. LOWER LIMBS: Rectus femoris, quadriceps, pectineum, adductors.

LEVEL AND GOALS:

- Moderate to advanced leve;
- Movement carried out in closed kinetic chain of the lower limbs;
- Perform movement in the sagittal plane;
- Promote activation of the anterior and backbone muscles of the spine due to the gravity action;
- Promote proprioceptive stimulation on the soles of the feet with the wall;
- Promote activation of the lateral muscles of the lumbar spine to stabilize the ball;
- Work balance;
- Posture performed on the wall generates a muscle force from the anterior chain of the body due to gravity.

SUPINE HIP AND SPINE FLEXION

POSITIONS AND ARTICULAR MOVEMENTS

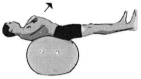

Fig. 241

- Cervical, thoracic and lumbar spine: Extension neutral in transition for flexion
- Shoulder: light bilateral flexion
- Elbow: bilateral flexion
- Wrist and fingers: slight flexion
- Hip: extension in transition to flexion
- Knee: bilateral extension
- Ankle: bilateral neutral position.

MOVEMENT EXECUTION: sitting on the ball with feet propped against the wall, the practitioner performs flexion and extension of the spine and hip, rolling the ball backwards, stopping the movement when the body is all in prone position.

ACTIVATED MUSCLES: TRUNK: Forehead straight and lateral straight head, long head and neck, bilateral (isometric) straight and transverse abdominal, bilateral internal and external oblique (stabilizers), spine erectors, Transespinalis. LOWER LIMBS: Protruding proximal portion, iliopsoas. (isotonic), adducts.

LEVEL AND GOALS:

- Advanced level;
- Movement with the level upgraded;
- Perform movement in the sagittal plane;
- Promote spinal mobilization in flexo-extension;
- Promote isotonic strengthening of the flexors and extensors of the spine;
- Promote isometric strengthening of the lateral muscles of the lumbar spine, by keeping the hip stabilized and the ball still;
- Promote activation of the hip flexor and adductor muscles;
- Promote proprioceptive stimulation in the soles of the feet with the wall.

FOOT RAISING WITH HAND SUPPORT

POSITIONS AND ARTICULAR MOVEMENTS

- Cervical, Thoracic and Lumbar Column: mild Flexion.
- Shoulder: flexion in transition to extension.
- Elbow: extension.
- Wrist and fingers: extension.
- Hip: flexion.
- Knee: flexion in transition to extension.
- Ankle: dorsal flexion in transition to plantar flexion.

Fig. 242

MOVEMENT EXECUTION: sitting on the ball with his feet and hands resting on the wall, the practitioner performs a plantar flexion of the feet and flexion of the hip and knee by withdrawing the foot support on the wall, sliding the ball towards the wall, back on the ball and raising the feet upwards extending the knee.

ACTIVATED MUSCLES: TRUNK: Anterior head and lateral rectus head, long head and neck, bilateral sternocleidomastoid (isometric) Straight and transverse abdominal, bilateral internal and external oblique (stabilizers), spinal erectors, transespinalis, abdomen. UPPER LIMBS: Anterior serratus, deltoid, coracobrachial, pectoralis major, Large dorsal, triceps, anecdotal, wrist extensors. LOWER LIMBS: Femoral straight, ilipsoas, vast, soleus, gastrognemio.

LEVEL AND GOALS:

- Advanced level;
- Perform sagging in the sagittal plane;
- Promote balance;
- Promote isometric activation and strengthening of the spinal and hip flexors;
- Promote activation and strengthening (isometric) of the lateral muscles of the lumbar spine by the stability of the ball;
- Promote isometric activation and strengthening of the horizontal adductors of the shoulders;
- Promote proprioceptive stimulation of the joints of the upper limbs;
- Promote active stretching of the hamstrings and erector of the lumbar spine.

UPSIDE DOWN SPIDER

POSITIONS AND ARTICULAR MOVEMENTS

- Cervical, thoracic and lumbar spine: extension in transition for flexion.

- Shoulder: transitional neutral extension for flexion with horizontal abduction.

- Elbow: extension in transition for flexion.

- Wrist and fingers: neutral position in transition for extension ending in neutral position holding the ball.

- Hip: flexion in transition to extension ending with flexion.

- Knee: full Flexion for Total Extension.

- Ankle: dorsal flexion to plantar flexion ending in the neutral position.

MOVEMENT EXECUTION: with the back on the ball, the practitioner performs a hyperextension of the spine, rolling the ball backwards by touching the hand on the wall, then withdraws one foot at a time from the ground leading to the wall with the hip and knee flexed to better position. The feet, once you have the four limbs resting on the wall, gradually withdraw your hand from the wall, leaving only the feet, finishing the posture with the extension of the knee and moving the ball away from the wall

ACTIVATED MUSCLES: TRUNK: Abdominal rectus (in the pull of the legs upwards leading to the wall). UPPER LIMBS: spine erector: anterior serratus, lower round, pectoralis major, deltoid lateral and posterior fibers, triceps, anecdotal, biceps long, coracobrachial. LOWER LIMBS: Iliopsoas, pectin, adductors, quadriceps (in the pull of the legs upwards leading to the wall).

LEVEL AND GOALS:

- Advanced level;
- Perform the movement in the sagittal plane;
- Promote mobilization of the hip and knee spine in extension and flexion, and extreme flexion of the cervical in the last posture;
- Promote elongation of the anterior chain in the second posture and posterior chain of the spine and lower limbs in the last posture;
- Increase blood flow to the head, venous return and lymphatic system;
- Work Balance and Body Consciousness.

(SARVÁNGÁSANA)

LEG RAISING WITH HIP ABDUCTION

POSITIONS AND ARTICULAR MOVEMENTS

Fig. 244

- Cervical, Thoracic and Lumbar Spine: flexion.

- Scapular belt: bilateral abduction.

- Shoulder: flexion with mild bilateral horizontal abduction.

- Elbow: bilateral extension.

- Handle: bilateral flexion in transition for extension only the hand resting on the wall.

- Hip: bilateral flexion and abduction in transition for extension beyond the raised leg.

- Knee: bilateral extension.

- Ankle: bilateral dorsal flexion in transition to plantar flexion only the raised leg.

MOVEMENT EXECUTION: with the support of the feet on the wall, legs abducted and with the hands in the lateral region of the legs, the practitioner removes one foot from the wall taking up, instead of the removed foot puts the hand to remain in the support.

ACTIVATED MUSCLES: TRUNK: Straight abdominal, oblique, erect spine to prevent body from falling back. UPPER LIMBS: Anterior serratile, pectoralis major, shoulder girdle muscles, coracobrachial, triceps and anchovy, biceps, wrist extensors (concentrically). LOWER LIMBS: Magnus, short and long adductors and ischiatibial adductors to keep the leg extended. Gluteus maximus acts to understand the hips, soleus and gastrognemius to do the plantar flexion.

LEVEL AND GOALS:

- Advanced level;
- Movement with a high degree of difficulty;
- Perform the movement in the sagittal plane;
- Promote spinal, hip and knee mobilization in extension and flexion and extreme flexion of the cervical in the last posture;
- Promote elongation of the posterior spine chain and adductors;

OBS.: Increase blood flow to the head, venous return and lymphatic system.

- Promote strengthening of high leg hip extensors;
- Work on concentration;
- Work the balance.

SAIL

POSITIONS AND ARTICULAR MOVEMENTS

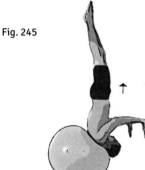

Fig. 245

- Cervical Spine Extension in transition for extreme flexion; Thoracic and Lumbar: slight flexion in transition for thoracic flexion and extension of the lumbar.

- Shoulder: horizontal abduction.

- Elbow: bilateral flexion.

- Wrist and fingers: extension.

- Hip: flexion in transition to extension.

- Knee: flexion in transition to extension.

- Ankle: bilateral plantar flexion.

MOVEMENT EXECUTION: with the back on the ball and with the hands on the wall, the practitioner performs an extension of the lumbar spine, the hip and the knee extending the legs upwards.

ACTIVATED MUSCLES: TRUNK: Straight abdominal, oblique, erect spine to prevent body from falling back. UPPER LIMBS: Anterior sawtooth, pectoralis major, shoulder girdle muscles, coracobrachial, triceps and anchovy, biceps, wrist extensors (concentrically). LOWER LIMBS: Magno, short and long and ischiatibial adductors to keep the legs together and extended. Maximo gluteus acts to extend the hips, soleus and gastrognemio to do the plantar flexion).

LEVEL AND GOALS:

- Advanced level;
- Perform movement performed in the sagittal plane;
- Promote mobilization of the hips, knees and lumbar spine and flexion-extension;
- Promote isometric strengthening of the scapular girdle muscles;
- Promote isometric strengthening of hip extensors and adductors;

OBS.: Due to gravity, venous return increases blood flow to the head area and increases intracranial pressure and lymphatic circulation.

- Promote elongation of cervical extensors;
- Work on concentration;
- Work the balance.

BOARD EDUCATION

The movements shown below were created to be performed with the use of the board. It is a work directed to the practitioners of boardsports, whose objective is to enable the practitioner to experience the movement in another medium to facilitate the memorization (motor and neural) of the specific movement of these sports. It is always good to observe some parts of the body during the movements, especially the knees, as we know boardsports can be harmful to the joints as they always work the maximum range of movement. Some movements follow the same lineage of the previous ones containing some information and others were placed only as illustrations to the movements.

HAND RAIL STRETCHING

Fig. 246

POSITIONS AND ARTICULAR MOVEMENTS

- Cervical, Thoracic and Lumbar Spine: neutral position of extension in transition for flexion.
- Shoulder: neutral position in transition for flexion.
- Elbow: slight flexion in transition to extension.
- Wrist and fingers: slight flexion.
- Hip: flexion.
- Knee: flexion in transition to extension.
- Ankle: neutral position in transition for dorsiflexion.

MOVEMENT EXECUTION: sitting on the ball the practitioner performs an exhalation and flexes the spine, extending the knees and performing a dorsiflexion placing the edge of the board on the ground and reaching with the hands.

ACTIVATED MUSCLES: TRUNK: Abdominal straight, oblique, erect spine eccentrically UPPER LIMBS: pectoralis major, Deltoid, coracobrachial, (concentrically). LOWER LIMBS: Quadriceps, Tibial anterior, eversores.

LEVEL AND GOALS:

- Basic level;
- Perform movement in the sagittal plane;
- Promote spinal mobilization in flexion;
- Promote activation of the spinal flexors;
- Promote stretching of spine extensors and knee flexors and plantar.

LAYBACK SIMULATION

Fig. 247

MOVEMENTS AND ARTICULAR POSITIONS

- Cervical column: neutral; Thoracic and Lumbar: neutral position in transition to extension.

- Shoulder: neutral position in transition for flexion o and extension.

- Elbow: extension in transition for slight flexion.

- Wrist and fingers: neutral in transition to extension.

- Hip: transition flexion for extension.

- Knee: flexion.

- Ankle: neutral position.

MOVEMENT EXECUTION: sitting on the ball with the shoulders in neutral position, the practitioner performs a spinal and hip extension movement by touching the back of the ball and placing one hand on the ground as a support, returning the initial position with the flexion of the spine and hip.

COMPLEX MOVEMENTS INVOLVING MULTIPLE JOINTS AND MULTIPLE MUSCLES

LEVEL AND GOALS:

- Perform movement in the oblique plane;
- Work on postural reactions. (Equilibrium, straightening and rectification);
- Mobilize the spine in slight rotation, extension and bending;
- Promote approach and removal of thighs with trunk;
- Simulate layback with hand on edge;
- Promote elongation of the spine and hip flexors;
- Simulate one of the surf moves performed.

GRAB RAIL SIMULATION

Fig. 248

POSITIONS AND ARTICULAR MOVEMENTS

- Cervical, Thoracic and Lumbar Spine: neutral position of extension in transition for flexion.
- Shoulder: transition neutral position for abduction.
- Elbow: extension in transition to light Flexion.
- Wrist and fingers: slight flexion.
- Hip: bilateral flexion in transition for extension of only one.
- Knee: fexion.
- Ankle: neutral position in transition for only one dorsiflexion.

MOVEMENT EXECUTION: sitting on the ball, the practitioner rotates the spine by leaning against the side of one of the thighs on the ball and one of the knees on the board with one hand on the edge of the board simulating a grab rail movement or from coast to wave.

COMPLEX MOVEMENTS INVOLVING MULTIPLE JOINTS AND MUSCLES

LEVEL AND GOALS:

- Basic to moderate level;
- Perform movement performed on the oblique plane;
- Promote spinal mobilization in flexion, hips, flexion-extension knees;
- Promote activation of the spinal flexors and rotators;
- Work balance and coordination;
- Work muscle memory by simulating movement.

CHANGE OF DIRECTIONS

Fig. 249

POSITIONS AND ARTICULAR MOVEMENTS

- Cervical, Thoracic and Lumbar Spine: neutral position of extension in transition for slight flexion.
- Shoulder: neutral position in transition for slight flexion
- Elbow: flexion in transition to extension.
- Wrist and fingers: slight flexion
- Hip: flexion
- Knee: flexion in transition for slight extension.
- Ankle: feutral position in transition for dorsiflexion.

MOVEMENT EXECUTION: sitting on the ball with the board in front of the ball, the practitioner performs a hip flexion accompanied by a rotation of the lower trunk, removing the board from the front and leading to the side of the ball, changing the direction of the board.

ACTIVATED MUSCLES: TRUNK: Abdominal straight, oblique, erect spine eccentrically. LOWER LIMBS: Hamstring, quadriceps, iliopsoas, short adductor.

LEVEL AND GOALS:

- Moderate level;
- Perform movement performed in the sagittal and transverse plane;
- Promote lower column mobilization in rotation;
- Work balance;
- Improve base change for kitesurfing;
- Promoting spinner and spinal flexor activation and flexors and knee extenders.

BASIC JUMP

Fig. 250

POSITIONS AND ARTICULAR MOVEMENTS

- Cervical, Thoracic and Lumbar Spine: neutral position of extension in transition for slight flexion.
- Shoulder: neutral position in transition for gentle bending.
- Elbow: flexion in transition to extension.
- Wrist and fingers: slight flexion.
- Hip: flexion.
- Knee: flexion.
- Ankle: feutral position in transition for dorsiflexion.

MOVEMENT EXECUTION: sitting on the ball, the practitioner performs a hip flexion by raising and removing the board from the ground, making a slight flexion of the spine, returning to the initial position, returned to the board in the ground.

ACTIVATED MUSCLES: TRUNK: Abdominal straight, oblique, erect spine eccentrically. UPPER LIMBS: Deltoid, pectoralis major, Deltoid, coracobrachial, (concentrically). LOWER LIMBS: Hamstrings, iliopsoas, short adductor, Tibial anterior, eversores.

LEVEL AND GOALS:

- Moderate level;
- Perform movement in the sagittal plane;
- Promote spinal mobilization in flexion;
- Work balance;
- Approximate the trunk to the thighs;
- Promote activation of the hip flexors and hip flexors.

BASIC JUMP WITH TAIL GRAB

Fig. 251

POSITIONS AND ARTICULAR MOVEMENTS

- Cervical, Thoracic and Lumbar Spine: neutral position of extension in transition for slight flexion.
- Shoulder: neutral position in transition for gentle bending.
- Elbow: flexion in transition to extension.
- Wrist and fingers: slight flexion.
- Hip: flexion.
- Knee: transition flexion to extend one of the knees.
- Ankle: neutral position in transition for dorsiflexion.

MOVEMENT EXECUTION: sitting on the ball, the practitioner performs a hip flexion by raising and removing the board from the ground, making a slight flexion of the spine, returning to the initial position, returned to the board in the ground.

ACTIVATED MUSCLES: TRUNK: Abdominal straight, oblique, erect spine eccentrically. UPPER LIMBS: Deltoid, pectoralis major, Deltoid, coracobrachial, (concentrically). LOWER LIMBS: Hamstrings, iliopsoas, short adductor, Tibial anterior, eversores.

LEVEL AND GOALS:

- Advanced level;
- Perform movement in the sagittal plane;
- Promote spinal mobilization in flexion;
- Work balance;
- Approximate the trunk to thighs;
- Promote activation of the hip flexors and hip flexors.

JUMP WITH GRAB RAIL

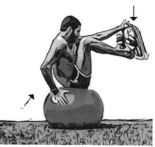

Fig. 252

PPOSITIONS AND ARTICULAR MOVEMENTS

- Cervical, Thoracic and Lumbar Spine: neutral position of extension in transition for slight flexion.

- Shoulder: neutral position in transition for gentle bending. One extends and the other flexes.

- Elbow: flexion in transition to one-sided extension.

- Wrist and fingers: slight flexion grabbing the rail and extension supported on the ball.

- Hip: bilateral flexion.

- Knee: bilateral flexion.

- Ankle: neutral position in transition for dorsiflexion

MOVEMENT EXECUTION: sitting on the ball, the practitioner performs a hip flexion and removes the plank from the floor, performing a slight flexion of the spine, approaching the thigh of the TRUNK and holding the board edge with one hand, returned to the board on the ground.

ACTIVATED MUSCLES: TRUNK: Abdominal straight, oblique, erect spine eccentrically. UPPER LIMBS: pectoralis major, Deltoid, coracobrachial, (concentrically). LOWER LIMBS: Hamstrings, iliopsoas, short adductor, Tibial anterior, eversores.

LEVEL AND GOALS:

- •Advanced level;
- Perform movement in the sagittal plane;
- Promote spinal mobilization in flexion;
- Work balance and coordination;
- Approximate the trunk to thighs;
- Facilitate the movement of picking up the board;
- Promote activation of the hip flexors and hip flexors.

GRAB RAIL VARIATIONS

Fig. 253　　　　　　Fig. 254　　　　　　Fig. 255

Fig. 256a　　　　　　Fig. 256b　　　　　　Fig. 257

BOARD APPROXIMATION AND DISTANCING

Fig. 258

POSITIONS AND ARTICULAR MOVEMENTS

- Cervical, Thoracic and Lumbar Spine: neutral position of extension in transition for flexion.

- Shoulder: horizontal abduction.

- Elbow: flexion of one and extension of the other.

- Wrist and fingers: neutral and extension (ground).

- Hip: flexion in transition to extension.

- Knee: flexion in transition to extension.

- Ankle: dorsiflexion.

MOVEMENT EXECUTION: in lateral decubitus, with the lower TRUNK and hip on the ball. With the hip and knee flexed, the hand on the ground supporting the weight and one end of the board on the ground, the practitioner performs an extension and flexion of the hips and knees. Approaching and moving thighs away in trunk.

ACTIVATED MUSCLES: TRUNK: abdominal straight, internal and external oblique, lumbar square, erect spine eccentrically. UPPER LIMBS: (Hand in the ground) rotator cuff, pectoralis major, lateral and anterior deltoid, coracobrachial, triceps. LOWER LIMBS: hamstrings, iliopsoas, adductors, abductors, anterior tibial and eversores.

LEVEL AND GOALS:

- Advanced level;

- Perform movement in the sagittal plane;

- Promote hip and knee mobilization in flexion and extension;

- Work balance;

- Work on the activation and strengthening of the shoulder girdle and shoulder with the hand on the ground;
- Approximate the trunk to thighs;
- Facilitate the movement of approaching the board;
- Promote activation of the spine flexors and hip and knee flexors.

ABDOMINAL KNEE FLEXION-EXTENSION KITE/SURF

Fig. 259

MOVEMENTS AND ARTICULAR POSITIONS

- Cervical spine: Thoracic and Lumbar flexion: slight flexion.
- Shoulder: bilateral extension.
- Elbow: bilateral Extension.
- Wrist and fingers: bilateral Extension.
- Hip: bilateral Flexion.
- Knee: extension in transition for flexion.
- Ankle: light dorsal flexion.

MOVEMENT EXECUTION: sitting on the ball with shoulders in hyperextension with hands on the ground and board in the foot, the practitioner performs a knee movement in alternating flexion and extension, taking the board up and down alternately.

ACTIVATED MUSCLES: TRUNK: rectus abdominis lower portion, obliquus internal and external. UPPER LIMBS: deltoid posterior fibers (rotator cuff) major and minor round, rhomboids, trapezius, triceps, anecdotal, wrist extensors and fingers (isometric). LOWER LIMBS: rectus femoris, iliopssoas, tensor of fascia to can, gluteus maximus, medium and minimum; adductors and plantar flexors (isometric).

LEVEL AND GOALS:

- Advanced level;
- Perform movement in the sagittal plane;
- Work on postural reactions. (balance, straightening and rectification);
- Promote isometric strengthening give trunk flexors;
- Promote passive stretching of the flexors of the shoulder and elbow flexors;
- Promote an isometric contraction of closed-arm shoulder extensors;
- Promote strengthening of hip flexors in open chain;
- Promote strengthening of the lower abdominal muscles.

SIDE SHIFT

Fig. 260

MOVEMENTS AND ARTICULAR POSITIONS

- Cervical column: Thoracic and Lumbar flexion: neutral position in transition for slight lateral flexion

- Shoulder: neutral position in transition for adduction and slight abduction.

- Elbow: extension.

- Wrist and fingers: neutral (solo) extension and finger flexion

- Hip: transition flexion for extension (only one hip).

- Knee: flexion in transition to extension (only one knee).

- Ankle: neutral position in transition for inversion and slight eversion.

MOVEMENT EXECUTION: sitting on the ball with the shoulders in neutral position, the practitioner performs a lateral movement of the hip extending one hip and one knee, placing one of the hands on the ground and the other at the end of the board, returning the lateral movement of the hip, returning to the starting position.

COMPLEX MOVEMENTS INVOLVING MULTIPLE JOINTS AND MUSCLES

LEVEL AND GOALS:

- Moderate level;
- Perform movement in the oblique plane;
- Work on postural reactions (balance, straightening and grinding);
- Promote dissociation of the shoulder girdle with the pelvic girdle;
- Simulate one of the moves performed on kitesurf.

HAND RAIL AIR SIMULATION

Fig. 261

MOVEMENTS AND ARTICULAR POSITIONS

- Cervical spine: Thoracic and Lumbar flexion: neutral position in transition for mild flexion, rotation and lateral flexion

- Shoulder: neutral position in transition for slight flexion o and abduction.

- Elbow: extension in transition for slight flexion

- Wrist and fingers: neutral in transition for flexion of fingers (plank) and extension (ground)

- Hip: flexion

- Knee: flexion in transition to stretch only one.

- Ankle: light dorsal flexion.

MOVEMENT EXECUTION: sitting on the ball with the shoulders in a neutral position, the practitioner performs a pushing motion upwards, withdrawing the board from the ground and turning the trunk over the ball keeping the hips flexed. One knee extended and the other flexed, placing one of the knees hands on the ground and the other on catching the edge of the board, returning the movement back to the starting position.

COMPLEX MOVEMENTS INVOLVING MULTIPLE JOINTS AND MULTIPLE MUSCLES

LEVEL AND GOALS:

- Advanced level;
- Perform movement in the oblique plane;
- Work on postural reactions (balance, straightening and grinding);
- Mobilize the spine in rotation and flexion;
- Promote thighs closer to trunk;
- Simulate the air with your hand on the edge;
- Simulate the aerial with the movements of the legs;
- Simulate one of the movements of the surf;
- Working with motor coordination.

VARIATIONS

Fig. 262

Fig. 263

Fig. 264

VARIAÇÕES DE ROTAÇÕES

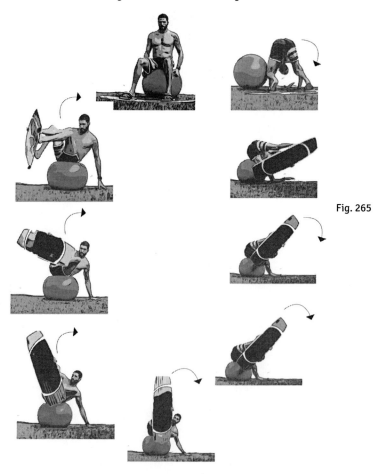

Fig. 265

REFERENCES:

BOOKS

_____. **Guia de Meditação**. 3. ed. Florianópolis: Dharma, 2001.

_____. **História do yoga**. 2. ed. Florianópolis: Dharma, 2000.

ABDALLAH, Achour. **Exercícios de Alongamento anatomia e fisiologia**. 1. ed. São Paulo: Manole, 2002.

AMARO, J.L.; GAMEIRO, M.O.O. **Incontinência Urinária:** Tratamento não cirúrgico cinesioterapia. Belo Horizonte: Atheneu, 2001.

AMERICAN COLEGE OF SPORTS MEDICINE. **Diretrizes do ACMS para os testes de esforço e sua prescrição**. 6. ed. Rio de Janeiro: Guanabara Koogan, 2003.

ANDREWS, James R.; HARRELSON, Gary L.; WILK, Kevin E. **Reabilitação Física do Atleta**. 3. ed. Rio de Janeiro: Elsiever, 2005.

AREIAS, Almir das. **O que é Capoeira**. São Paulo: Brasiliense, 1983.

ASCHER, C. **Variações de Postura na criança**. São Paulo: Manole, 1976.

BARRETO, D. **Dança; Ensino, sentimentos e possibilidades na escola**. São Paulo: Autores autorizados LTDA, 2004.

BORGES, D. *et al.* **Aspectos clínicos e práticos da reabilitação**. 1. ed. São Paulo: Artes Médicas, 2007.

CAMINADA, E. **História da dança**: evolução cultural. Rio de Janeiro: Sprint, 1999.

CARPENTER, Carlos Sandro. **Biomecânica**. Rio de Janeiro: Sprint, 2005.

CARRIÈRE, Beate. **Bola Suíça**: Teoria, exercícios básicos e aplicação clínica. São Paulo: Manole, 1999.

CARVALHO, M. A. P. **Noções práticas de reumatologia.** 2. ed. Belo Horizonte: Health, 1998. p. 301-312.

CARVALHO, M. A. P.; REGO, R. R. **Fibromialgia**: 2. ed. São Paulo: Medsi, 2001.

COHEN, M. ABDALLA, RJ. **Lesões no esporte – Diagnóstico – Prevenção – Tratamento.** Rio de Janeiro: Revinter, 2003.

CRAIG, Collen. **Abdominais com a Bola.** 2. ed. São Paulo: Phorte, 2006.

CRAIG, Collen. **Pilates com a Bola.** 2. ed. São Paulo: Phorte, 2005.

CRAIG, Collen. **Treinamento de força com bola.** 2. ed. São Paulo: Phorte, 2007.

DANGELO, J. G.; FATTINI, C. A. **Anatomia Básica dos sistemas orgânicos.** São Paulo: Atheneu, 1997.

DAVID L. NELSON; MICHAEL M. COX. **Lehninger Principles of Biochemistry.** 3. ed. New York: Worth Publishing, 2001.

DENADAI, S. B; GRECO, C. C. **Prescrição do treinamento aeróbico: Teoria e Prática.** Rio de Janeiro: Koogan, 2005.

ELIADE, Mircéa. **Patañjali e o yoga.** Lisboa/Rio de Janeiro: Relógio D' Água editores, 2000.

FEUERSTEIN, Georg. **A Tradição do yoga.** 4. ed. São Paulo: Pensamento, 1998.

FEUERSTEIN, Georg. **Uma Visão Profunda do yoga.** 2. ed. São Paulo: Pensamento, 2005.

FREITAS, L. J. **Capoeira infantil**: a arte de brincar com o próprio corpo. Curitiba: Gráfica Expoente, 1997.

FRITZ, Sandy; PAHOLSKY, Kathleen M. **Terapia pelo movimento.** 1. ed. São Paulo: Manole, 2002.

GRAY, D. Goss, C. M. **Anatomia.** Rio de Janeiro: Guanabara Koogan, 1998.

GUYTON, A. C. **Fisiologia Humana**. 6. ed. Rio de Janeiro: Guanabara Koovan, 1998.

GUYTON, Arthur C. **Fisiologia humana e mecanismos das doenças**. 5. ed. Rio de Janeiro: Guanabara Koogan, 1993.

HALL, Carrie. M.; BRODY, Lori. T. **Exercícios Terapêuticos na busca função**. Rio de Janeiro: Guanabara Koogan, 2001.

HALL, S. **Biomecânica Básica**. Rio de Janeiro: Guanabara Koogan, 1993.

HALL, Susan J. **Biomecânica Básica**. 5. ed. São Paulo: Manole, 2009.

HAMILL, J.; KNUTZEN, M. K. **Bases Biomecânica do Movimento Humano**. São Paulo: Manole, 1999.

HERMÓGENE, José Hermógenes. **Saúde Plena**: yogaterapia. Rio de Janeiro: Nova Era, 2001.

HOFFMAN, S. J.; HARRIS, J. C. **Cinesiologia:** O estudo da Atividade Física. Porto Alegre: Artmed, 2002.

IYENGAR, B. K. S. **A árvore do ioga**. São Paulo: Globo, 2001.

IYENGAR, B. K. S. **A Luz da Ioga**. 6. ed. São Paulo: Globo, 2003.

JACOB, S. W. **Anatomia e Fisiologia Humana**. 5. ed. Rio de Janeiro: Guanabara Koogan, 1992.

KAPANDJI, A. I. **Fisiologia articular, membros superiores**. 6. ed. São Paulo: Guanabara Koogan, 2000.

KAPANDJI, A. I. **Fisiologia articular, membros inferiores**. 6. ed. São Paulo: Guanabara Koogan, 2006.

KAPANDJI, A. I. **Fisiologia articular, tronco e coluna vertebral**. 5. ed. São Paulo: Guanabara Koogan, 2000.

KENDALL, Peterson F. **Músculos, Provas e funções**. 5. ed. São Paulo: Manole, 2007.

KISNER, C. **Exercícios Terapêuticos, fundamentos e técnicas**. 4. ed. São Paulo: Manole, 2005.

KUPFER, Pedro. **Yoga Prático**. 3. ed. Florianópolis: Dharma, 2001.

LEONARD, C. T. **The Neuroscience of Human Movement.** USA: Mosby-Year Book, 1997.

LIPPERT, Lynn. **Cinesiologia clínica para fisioterapeutas:** Incluindo teste para auto-avaliação. 1. ed. Rio de Janeiro: Revinter, 1996.

LOPES, A. L. L. **A Capoeiragem no Rio de Janeiro**. Rio de Janeiro: Europa, 2000.

MARTNS, Daniela S.; CRUZ Tirciane M.F. **Exercícios com a bola Um Guia prático**. São Paulo: Phorte, 2007.

MAUGHAN, RON; GLEESON, MICHAEL; GREENHAFF, PAUL L. **Bioquímica do exercício e treinamento**. 1. ed. São Paulo: Manole, 2000. 240 p.

MIRANDA, Edalton. **Bases de Anatomia e Cinesiologia**. 6. ed. Rio de Janeiro: Sprint, 2006.

MOLINE, B. **Avaliação Médica e Física para Atletas e praticantes de Atividade Física**. 1. ed. São Paulo: Roca, 2000.

MOORE, K. L., DALLEY, A. F. **Anatomia orientada para clínica**. 4. ed. Rio de Janeiro: Guanabara Koogan, 1994.

MOREIRA, C. **Noções práticas de reumatologia**, volume I. Belo Horizonte: Health,1996. p. 26.

NEUMANN, Donald A. **Cinesiologia do aparelho músculo esquelético**. Fundamentos para a Reabilitação Física. Rio de Janeiro: Guanabara Koogan, 2005.

PEREIRA, Benedito. **Metabolismo celular e exercício físico**: aspectos bioquímicos e nutricionais. São Paulo: Phorte, 2004.

PLATONOV, V. **El entrenamiento desportivo**. Teoría y metodologia. Barcelona: Paindotribo, 1995.

PORTINARI, M. B. **História da dança**. Rio de Janeiro: Nova Fronteira S/A, 1989.

RANGEL, N. B. C. **Dança educação, educação física**; Proposta de ensino da dança e o universo da educação física. 1. ed. São Paulo: Fontoura, 2002.

RASCH, P. **Cinesiologia e Anatomia aplicada**. 7. ed. Rio de Janeiro: Guanabara, Koogan, 1991.

RASCH, P. J.; BURKE, Roger K. **Cinesiologia e Anatomia Aplicada**. 5. ed. Rio de Janeiro: Guanabara Koogan, 1983.

ROBISON, Lynner; NAPPER, Howard. **Exercícios inteligentes com Pilates e yoga**. 11. ed. São Paulo: Pensamento, 2006.

ROCHA, Ruth. **Minidicionário**. São Paulo: Scipione, 1996.

RUBINSTEIN, I. **Clínicas Brasileiras de urologia incontinência urinária na mulher**. v. 1. Belo Horizonte: Atheneu, 2001.

SENNA, Carlos. "Capoeira, Arte Marcial Brasileira". **Cadernos de Cultura**, n. 1, 1980.

SILVA, G. O. **Capoeira do engenho à universidade**. São Paulo: Cepesup, 1993.

SMITH, L. K. *et al*. **Cinesiologia Clínica de Brunnstrom**. 5. ed. São Paulo: Manole, 1997.BRITO

SOBOTTA. **Atlas da Anatomia Humana**. Cabeça, pescoço e extremidade superior. 21. ed. v. 1. Rio de Janeiro: Guanabara Koogan, 2000.

SOBOTTA. **Atlas da Anatomia Humana**. Troncas vísceras e extremidades inferiores. 21. ed. v. 1. Rio de Janeiro: Guanabara Koogan, 2000.

SOUZA. J. C. **Mestres Bimba**: Corpo de Mandiga, Manati: Rio de Janeiro, 2002.

SPENCE, Alexandre P. **Anatomia Humana Básica**. 2. ed. São Paulo: Manole, 1991.

STARKET, Chad. **Recursos Terapêuticos em Fisioterapia**. 1. ed. São Paulo: Manole, 2001.

THOMPSON, C. W.; FLOYD, R. T. **Manual de Cinesiologia Estrutural**. 12. ed. São Paulo: Manole, 1997.

VERDERI, Erica. **Treinamento Funcional com bola**. 1. ed. São Paulo: Phorte, 2008.

VIEIRA, L. R. **O Jogo de Capoeira**: Cultura Popular no Brasil. 2. ed. Rio de Janeiro: Sprint, 1998.

WESINSTEIN, Stuart L. **Ortopedia de Turek Princípios e Aplicações**. 1. ed. São Paulo: Manole, 2000.

WHITING, W.; ZERNICKE, R. **Biomecânica da Lesão músculo esquelética**. Rio de Janeiro: Guanabara Koogan, 2001.

WINTER, D. A. **Biomechanicals and Motor Control of Human Movement**. 4. ed. Canada: Wiley, 2009.

SCIENTIFIC PAPERS

ALEJANDRO, D. P. Efectos del Hatha-yoga sobre la salud. Parte II. **Revista Cubana Med. Gen. Integr.**, Ciudad de La Habana, v. 14, n. 5, sep./oct. 1998.

AMANAJÁS, D. C. Distrofia Muscular. **Fisio & terapia**, Rio de Janeiro, ano 7, n. 39, p. 11-14, jun./jul., 2003.

CASTRO J. L. VITOR. Capoeira e os diversos aprendizados no espaço escolar. **Revista Motrivivência**, ano 11, n. 14, p. 159-171, maio 2000.

CASPERSEN, C. J.; POWELL, K. E.; CRISTENSON, G. M. Physical activity, exercise and physical finess: definition and distinctions for health-relates research. **Public Health Reports**, v. 100, n. 2, p. 126-131, 1985.

CRUZ, L. S.; GUIMARÃES, L. S. Exercícios Terapêuticos: A cinesiologia como importante recurso de fisioterapia. **Revista Lato & Sensu,** Belém, v. 4, n. 1, p. 3-5, out. 2003.

GONÇALVES, G. A. C.; GONÇALVES, A. K.; JUNIOR, A. P. Desenvolvimento motor na teoria dos sistemas dinâmicos. **Revista Matriz**, v. 1 n. 1, jun. 1995.

KRISCHKE, A. M. A.; SOUZA, I. S. Dança Improvisação, Uma Relação a Ser Trilhada com o Lúdico. **Artigo Motricidade**, ano XVI, n. 23, p. 15-27, dez. 2004.

LEITE. F. H. C; Contato improvisação (Contact improvisation) um Diálogo em Dança. **Artigo Movimento**, Porto Alegre, v. 11, n. 2, p. 89-110, maio/ago. 2005.

LOPES, C. H. C; GHIRITTO, F. M. S; MATSUDO, S. M.; ALMEIDA, V. S. Efeitos de um programa de 6 semanas de exercícios na bola suíça sobre a percepção da dor lombar em estudantes de educação física. **Revista brasileira de ciência e movimento**, Editora universa, São Paulo, v. 14, n. 4, p. 15-21, jun. 2006.

SANCHEZ, E.; MARQUES A. Origem e evolução da fisioterapia: aspectos históricos e legais. **Revista Brasileira da USP**, São Paulo v. 1, jul./dez. 1994.

STEFANELLO, T. D. Uso de shiatsu como recursos alternativos em pacientes lombalgicos. 2007. Disponível em: <https://www.toshiroms.com.br>.

VINHAS. C. Arte do contato-improvisação. **Revista Dança em revista**, São Paulo, ano 1, n. 2, jan. 2007.

MASTERS, DISSERTATIONS AND FINAL COURSE MONOGRAPHS

CASSOL, R.; BERTONCELLO, I. **Análise ergonômica da Bola suíça em fisioterapia.** 2009. Monografia (Fisioterapia) – Faculdade de Assis Gurgacz/FAG, Cascavel (PR), 2009.

CHADE, L. O. **Formação de Público para a Dança:** O Papel das companhias de Dança na Educação para a Cultura. Trabalho de Conclusão de Curso de Pós-graduação de Projetos Culturais e Organização de Eventos produzidos sob orientação da Profa. Dra. Soledad Galhardo. CELÁCC/ECA-USP, 2009.

D'AGOSTINI, A. **O jogo da capoeira no contexto antropológico e biomecânico.** 2004. Dissertação (Mestrado) – Pós-Graduação em Educação Física da Universidade Federal de Santa Catarina, Florianópolis, SC, 2004.

FERREIRA, E. A. G.; Marques, A. P. **Postura e controle postural:** desenvolvimento e aplicação de método quantitativo de avaliação postural. 2006. Tese (Doutorado) – Universidade de São Paulo, São Paulo, 2006.

FRIGERIO, Alejandro. **The Search for Africa:** Proustian Nostalgia in Afro-Brazilian Studies. 1989. Dissetação (Mestrado) – Universidade da Califórnia, Los Angeles, 1989.

KRISCHKE, A. M. A.; SOUZA, I. S. **Dança Improvisação, Uma Relação a Ser Trilhada com o Lúdico**. Anexo. Monografia defendida no curso de especialização em educação física escolar da CDS/UFSC. Florianópolis, 2004.

SANTOS, J. R. dos. **Yoga Educacional:** integração corpo e mente no processo de desenvolvimento da criança. Monografia defendida no curso de Educação Física da UFSC. Florianópolis, 2004.

WETLER, E. C. B. **Efeitos de um programa de ginástica postural sobre indivíduos com hérnia de disco lombar**. 2004. Dissertação (Mestrado) – Faculdade de Ciências da Saúde da Universidade de Brasília, Brasília, 2004.

INTERNET

FOLHA de S. PAULO de 29/01/2000, **Caderno Acontece**, Especial: p. 4. Disponível em <http://www.videodança.wordpress.com/ideokinesiscontato-improvisacaodanca-contemporenea>. Acesso em: 27 de mar. 2011.

VALERIO, M. **Arte**. Net. Outubro de 2001. Disponível em <www.xr.pro.br/arte.html>. Acesso em: 09 maio 2011.